WHY
FOUR
GOSPELS?

WHY FOUR GOSPELS?

The Historical Origins of the Gospels

DAVID ALAN BLACK

kregel
PUBLICATIONS

Grand Rapids, MI 49501

To the memory of William R. Farmer—
scholar, colleague, friend.

Why Four Gospels? The Historical Origins of the Gospels

© 2001 by David Alan Black

Published by Kregel Publications, a division of Kregel, Inc., P.O. Box 2607, Grand Rapids, MI 49501. For more information about Kregel Publications, visit our Web site: www.kregel.com.

ISBN 0-8254-2070-9

Printed in the United States of America

1 2 3 / 05 04 03 02 01

Contents

Preface 7

1. The Development of the Gospels 13

The Jerusalem Phase | 15

The Gentile Mission Phase | 20

The Roman Phase | 25

The Johannine Supplement | 30

Conclusion | 32

2. The Origins of the Gospels 35

The Principal Patristic Witnesses | 37

Evaluation of the Patristic Witnesses | 42

An Evaluation of Markan Priority | 47

The Credibility of the Fourfold-Gospel Hypothesis | 59

Conclusion | 62

3. The Making of the Gospels 65

The Composition of Matthew | 66

Luke's Use of Matthew | 69

CONTENTS

The Markan Synthesis | 76

The Background of John | 85

Conclusion | 90

Postscript 93

Bibliography 95

Index 113

Preface

To a biblical scholar this book may appear very elementary, if not banal. But it is not written for biblical scholars. During the course of my teaching a number of students have asked me to compose for them a brief, clear, and easily understandable summary of my beliefs regarding the historical origins of the Gospels. This matter was causing them concern and anxiety since it often seemed that proponents of higher criticism were undermining the historical value of the Gospels. In answer to this request, I composed a handout that was copied for private circulation. But as my views became more widely known, a number of friends thought that what I had written for my students might prove useful for pastors and laypeople whose occupations precluded an in-depth study of the matter. It is to meet the needs of such readers that I give this brief sketch to the public.

That such a treatment should be necessary today is obvious in light of the abuse of the historical-critical method by certain Gospel critics. Scarcely admissible philosophical and theological principles have often come to be mixed with this method. These principles have vitiated the method itself, as well as the conclusions derived from it. Some proponents of higher criticism have been led astray by the prejudicial views of rationalism, refusing to admit the existence of a supernatural order and the intervention of a personal God in the world through special revelation, miracles, and prophecies. Others begin with a false idea of faith, as if faith had nothing to do with historical truth or were even incompatible with it. Others deny the historical value and nature of the Gospels almost *a priori*. Finally, others make light of or reject outright the authority of the apostles as witnesses to Christ and their task and influence in the early church, extolling rather the creative power of the "community." These presuppositions are not only opposed to Christian doctrine, but are also devoid of scientific basis and alien to the correct principles of higher criticism.

This volume is an attempt to correct such aberrations. It seeks to renew, restore, and strengthen faith in the truth of the Gospels by providing scientific support for the church's continuous teaching on their apostolicity and historicity, namely that the Holy Spirit guided first Matthew, then Paul and his companion Luke, then Peter and his companion Mark, and finally John the apostle to hand on to the church during their own lifetime the Gospel given them by Jesus.

My chief debt in preparing this volume is to my esteemed colleague and friend Bernard Orchard of the Gospel Research Institute in Ealing Abbey, London, whose approach to the synoptic problem is a variation of the well-known Two-Gospel Hypothesis held by William Farmer and his circle. Although it was Dr. Orchard who originally suggested the term "Two-Gospel Hypothesis" to Farmer at the Society of Biblical Literature meeting in New York some twenty-five years ago in order to distinguish it from the more elementary Griesbach Hypothesis, he did not realize until recently that in Farmer's *International Bible Commentary* the Two-Gospel Hypothesis was given no ascertainable content beyond arguing for the order Matthew–Luke–Mark, thus minimizing the significance of the patristic evidence for the apostolicity and historicity of the Gospels. In fairness to everyone concerned, and to enable other scholars to distinguish his position from the Two-Gospel Hypothesis as propounded by Farmer and his colleagues, Orchard chose to call his view the Fourfold-Gospel Hypothesis, based on a term used by Irenaeus (*Against Heresies* 3.2.8) and in Vatican II's *Dei Verbum* (§18), because with the support of the patristic evidence it satisfactorily demonstrates the relationships between the four accounts of the one Gospel of Christ and thereby reveals the chronology of the life and messiahship of Jesus.

During a visit to Ealing Abbey in November 2000, Dr. Orchard and I discussed the possibility of publishing a brief volume that would introduce students and pastors to the Fourfold-Gospel Hypothesis. Our original thought—that of co-authoring a book on Gospel origins—was ultimately deemed unfeasible in view of Dr. Orchard's pressing professional and clerical duties. He therefore asked me if I would consider producing a popular digest of his views designed for circulation in colleges and seminaries. Since I had been teaching these views for many years and suspected that such a digest would immediately find an enthusiastic audience among students, I assented to his request, with the sole proviso that I would have unrestricted access to (and permission to quote from and summarize) his previously published works, most of which, however, were written for the scholarly guild and not for a general readership.

The present volume is, therefore, a unique work. While representing my own convictions about the synoptic problem, it is essentially a popularization of Dr. Orchard's views, written at his behest and with an eye on a hitherto unreached audience. It makes no claim to originality in any important matter, and the expert reader, into whose hands it should chance to fall, will recognize my indebtedness to the writings of Dr. Orchard on every page. The bibliography and footnotes indicate where my chief conscious debt lies. It should not be assumed, of course, that Dr. Orchard would agree with everything written here, nor is he to be held responsible for any errors or oversights this book may contain. In particular, I have taken the liberty of producing my own fresh translations of the church fathers from the original Greek and Latin, translations that differ in a number of particulars from those published by Dr. Orchard. Nevertheless, I am convinced that students will find within these pages a fair and accurate representation of the Fourfold-Gospel Hypothesis in all of its salient features.

The debts of gratitude that I wish to acknowledge are great and numerous. Andrew Neamtu and Abidan Shah, my personal assistants, gave meticulous and unstinting care to this work alongside their numerous other responsibilities in my office. Without their willingness to take on massive workloads, the task of finishing this manuscript alongside other heavy teaching and preaching commitments would simply have been too much. They were ably assisted by the considerable talents, accurate eye, and ever-ready help of my secretary, Phyllis Keith. Her cheerful attention to myriad details was invaluable as an impetus to complete this work.

Jim Weaver of Kregel Academic has been a ready source of help, encouragement, and good advice. I have valued my very close working relationship with Jim for many years. Likewise I appreciated the time I spent translating the fathers at Ealing Abbey in London, a trip made possible through a generous travel grant from Southeastern Seminary. I am grateful to President Paige Patterson and Dean Russ Bush for supporting me in this way and for the privilege of teaching in an institution that values research and writing. I should particularly like to record my thanks to Dr. Orchard for his impetus in launching this project and for his constant encouragement and enthusiastic support. Finally, I want to thank Professor Keith Elliott of the University of Leeds and Dr. Larry Kreitzer of the University of Oxford for inviting me to lecture in their respective institutions, where I was able to put forth a renewed defense of the trustworthiness of the patristic testimonies for New Testament studies. It is my sincere hope that this volume will challenge a future generation of Bible students to rethink the synoptic problem in light of the testimony of these early Christian witnesses.

Wake Forest, North Carolina
March 2001

The Development of the Gospels

THE CHRISTIAN CHURCH has always held that the four Gospels are the most important part of the written tradition handed on by the twelve apostles by virtue of their personal knowledge of Jesus acquired during their instruction by him in the course of his earthly mission. How and why the Gospels came to be written has, however, become a matter of controversy during the past two hundred years. Nevertheless, patient investigation enables us today to formulate a hypothesis that does justice both to critical scholarship and to the integrity of the ancient church fathers who first recorded the fundamental facts.

In its original sense the Gospel was not a literary product but the message of salvation that Jesus Christ brought as God's eschatological bearer of good news and that the early church understood, in keeping with the situation after Easter, as the word of salvation about Jesus Christ, crucified, risen, and exalted at the right hand of God. This proclamation of salvation was later committed to writing in books known as "Gospels," to record and attest Jesus' words and works and his death and resurrection and to present them as necessary for the acceptance of faith.

The fact that these new writings had a special and unique purpose brought with it the creation of a special literary genre.[1] Thus Mark's Gospel opens with the words: "The beginning of the gospel *(euangeliou)* of Jesus Christ" (Mark 1:1), meaning that the good news of what God has done in and through Jesus Christ would now be proclaimed to all nations (cf. Mark 13:10). While neither Matthew nor Luke begins in the same way as Mark, their basic message is identical. In Matthew Jesus proclaims "the gospel *(euangelion)* of the kingdom" (Matt 4:23; 9:35; 24:14), and in Luke the verbal form *euangelizomai* ("to proclaim the good news") is used to describe this activity (Luke 8:1; 16:16). Although the primary message of John's Gospel is identical to that of the Synoptic Gospels, neither the noun *euangelion* nor the verb *euangelizomai* appears. However, in 1 John (1:5; 3:11) the related term *angelia* ("message") is used, which may have been the Johannine designation for what we know as the Gospel according to John.

Since the Enlightenment, biblical criticism has been engaged with the synoptic problem and has offered a striking number of tensions and indeed "contradictions" between these Gospels. But these investigations of the synoptic problem entailed, and still entail, the danger of obscuring the common structural elements of the four canonical Gospels. Christian antiquity here affords a healthier perspective. Thus, for Irenaeus the fourfold canon of the Gospels represented a profoundly significant fact, foreseen and willed by God. He therefore spoke of the *tetramorphon* Gospel (*Against Heresies* 3.2.8)—the "tetramorphic" or "fourfold" Gospel.

---

1. Cf. F. Watson, *Text and Truth* (Grand Rapids: Eerdmans, 1997), 89 n. 7: "The title *euangelion kata* . . . indicates that, for their readers, the gospels did not constitute a 'sub-type' of an existing genre but a new genre. This would of course not be a *creatio ex nihilo:* the gospels may employ many of the conventions of the Hellenistic *bios,* without erasing the difference implied by the substitution of *euangelion* for *bios* in their titles."

By this he meant that each of the four Gospel accounts, and all of them together, have a common message as documents of faith in the service of faith. The differences between them, significant though they are, do not obscure their basic message of salvation through Christ.

The Spirit-directed process of inscripturating this fourfold Gospel involved four main phases—four turning points at each of which a suitable Gospel statement was found to be necessary for its proper growth.[2] These stages were the following:

1. The Jerusalem phase (Acts 1–12) under the leadership of Peter.
2. The Gentile mission phase (Acts 13–28) under the leadership of Paul.
3. The Roman phase requiring joint action by Peter and Paul.
4. The Johannine supplement.

Chapter 1 discusses these four stages in chronological order; and chapter 2 evaluates the historical evidence for these stages.

The Jerusalem Phase (A.D. 30–42; Acts 1–12)

According to the divine plan of salvation, the Messiah was not to appear until the times and circumstances were right. Among the circumstances that set the stage for the Messiah's coming were the following:

1. The existence of the Septuagint, an excellent Greek version of the sacred writings of the Jews (the Old Testament). After the resurrection of Christ, the Septuagint became the Bible of the Christian church and a powerful instrument for

---

2. The following discussion is indebted to B. Orchard, *The Evolution of the Gospels* (London: Ealing Abbey, n.d.), 1–17.

conveying to the whole world the knowledge of the true God that had already been given to the Jews.

2. The *Diaspora* (dispersion) of the Jews, along with their synagogues in all the main centers of the Roman Empire that had Greek as its common language, making the spread of the Jewish religion and way of life available to all educated and interested persons.

3. The *Pax Romana* (Roman Peace), which gave Christianity the opportunity to take firm root during the lifetime of the twelve apostles, whose function it was, as the principal witnesses of the Lord's life, death, and resurrection, to proclaim all that he had taught them.

These prerequisites having been met, the nascent church in Jerusalem was ready to missionize in the name of the risen Christ. The descent of the Holy Spirit upon the apostles and the 120 in the upper room on the day of Pentecost gave them confidence to go forth and preach all they had learned from Jesus. Their first task, under the direction of Peter, was to agree on the minimum organization necessary to undertake their world mission; and the Acts of the Apostles reveals to us that from the very beginning the Jerusalem church enjoyed the good order that came from a right understanding of the mind of Christ. The twelve apostles were the supreme authority by virtue of being the eyewitnesses personally selected by Jesus to control the expansion of the church, which was a living organism entirely independent of the theocratic state of Judaism and responsible to no one but God himself. And while esteeming the temple of God because of its historical associations, they were obliged to set up their own house churches (e.g., the church in the house of John Mark's mother), where they were able to celebrate the uniquely Christian ceremony of "breaking of bread," as bequeathed to them by Jesus.

The apostles' insistence on exact adherence to their teaching about Jesus led to the immediate emergence of a fellowship (based on baptism into Christ) that distinguished them from all other citizens of Jerusalem. Jesus himself, together with his Father and his Holy Spirit—the one triune God—was now the object of worship in the apostolic community of the church of Jerusalem. But this "alien body" of followers of Jesus had to justify its existence in the face of the fierce hostility from unconverted Sadducees, Pharisees, Levites, and high priests.

As soon as the first wave of converts had been baptized and their instruction organized by the Twelve, the apostles' thoughts turned to the practical question of how to unify and consolidate their teaching about Jesus. The apostles realized that they somehow needed to promulgate those passages of the Holy Scriptures from "Moses and all the prophets" (Luke 24:27) that Jesus had explained to Cleopas on the road to Emmaus. It also became clear to them that their main apologetic task was to demonstrate to the Jewish authorities that Jesus had literally fulfilled all the prophecies about the Messiah. These considerations were the original motivation for the composition of the Gospel of Matthew.

The Acts of the Apostles provides the necessary background information that enables us to see that the Gospel of Matthew was the ideal instrument to refute the calumnies about Jesus that the high priests were circulating. Matthew's Gospel met all the apologetic needs of the Jerusalem church in the years immediately following the resurrection when its doctrines were under attack—namely, Jesus' ancestry as a son of David, his being born of a virgin, his birth in Bethlehem, his commendation by John the Baptist, his miracles, his teaching with authority in the temple, his coming to fulfill the law of Moses and not to destroy it, his suffering like the Servant of Isaiah, his rejection by his own nation, and his miraculous resurrection from the dead.

All of the above elements of the Jesus story had long been foreshadowed in the sacred writings of the Jews. But how was all this and a great deal more to be reduced to the compass of one commercial scroll of thirty feet (ten meters), the standard length of a book, if the disciples were to travel "light" in compliance with their master's explicit instructions? The assistance of the Holy Spirit was indeed necessary if the essentials of the life and teaching of a man of Jesus' eminence were ever to be completely told. Christian tradition tells us that the Twelve entrusted this important work to the apostle Matthew; and so, not long after the resurrection, Matthew set to work. As his Gospel was meant to be a handbook for teaching and administration in the church, Matthew's purpose seems to have been to compile schematically the master's teachings without special regard to chronological order. Perhaps the greatest problem that he faced was to reduce to a manageable quantity the immense mass of material available to the Twelve in the form of personal reminiscences about the Lord. Matthew did not take this challenge lightly; and in order to produce a work worthy of proclaiming the Lord's glory he made skillful use of all five literary forms that were then the hallmark of good writing in the Hellenistic world: the proverb (or maxim), the narrative, the parable, the anecdote (*chreia* or short story), and the reminiscence (*apomnēmoneuma* or longer story).

The use of these Greek literary forms is an important indication that Matthew composed his work in Greek.[3] In any case, since Greek was the common language of communication throughout the Roman Empire and beyond, and with the Septuagint as the successful precedent, the Greek tongue was the obvious medium

---

3. On the problematic statement of Papias that Matthew wrote his Gospel *hebraidi dialektō,* see chapter 2.

for the effective presentation of the universal Gospel message.[4] Although highly educated, Matthew naturally experienced difficulty expressing himself in a foreign language and so betrayed his Palestinian origin in the style of the original Greek text, which contains many signs of his native Semitic tongue and thinking.[5]

With the help of the Holy Spirit and the rest of the Twelve, Matthew arranged the material he selected in three main sections:

1. The origin of Jesus through the opening of his public ministry in Galilee (1:1–4:17).
2. Jesus' Galilean ministry (4:18–18:35)—containing the bulk of his teaching—to which is attached a brief interlude in Transjordan (19:1–20:34).
3. All the Jerusalem events of Jesus' public mission, including the passion, death, and resurrection narratives (21:1–28:20).

Matthew's account of the infancy of Jesus is mostly apologetic, its aim being to prove that Jesus was conceived by the Holy Spirit, born of the virgin Mary, and the legitimate son of David by adoption by Joseph. The main part of the teaching of Jesus is given in a series of carefully crafted sermons designed to give the reader the clearest possible view of the way in which the Messiah, depicted as the Redeemer of the world, set out his implementation and supplementation of the old law. Thus the Sermon on the

---

4. Cf. M. Müller, *The First Bible of the Church: A Plea for the Septuagint* (Sheffield: Academic Press, 1996). On the most important differences between Classical Greek and the Koine of the New Testament, see D. A. Black, *Linguistics for Students of New Testament Greek* (2d ed.; Grand Rapids: Baker, 1995), 156–62.
5. The more common Semitic expressions found in the New Testament are discussed in D. A. Black, "New Testament Semitisms," *Bible Translator* 39 (1988): 215–23.

Mount (5:1–7:29) is constructed to give the reader the full power and beauty of the new spirit infused by Jesus into the old letter of the law of Moses. Further teachings are arranged in a series of four other discourses:

1. The missionary discourse (10:1–42).
2. The parables discourse (13:1–58).
3. The community discourse (18:1–35).
4. The eschatological discourse (24:1–25:46).

In short, then, the Gospel of Matthew was the manifesto of the mother church of Jerusalem and is therefore the fundamental document of the Christian faith. It was the chronicle that each of the apostles needed to take with him to his own distant field of evangelization and also the one that Paul was to take with him on his own missionary journeys and from which he appears to quote in 1 Thessalonians 4–5.[6] A savage persecution of the church, begun by Herod Agrippa I in 42, was the impetus for the dispersion of the apostles now possessing in the Gospel of Matthew the necessary instrument to support and confirm their preaching, while at the same time preserving their theological unity. The first phase was completed, and the second phase of the church's expansion was about to begin with the mission of Paul.

The Gentile Mission Phase (A.D. 42–62; Acts 13–28)

At the very beginning the apostles and their disciples had been content to preach only to Jews and God-fearers (pagans who believed in the truth of Judaism). But three events that occurred

---

6. See B. Orchard, "Thessalonians and the Synoptic Gospels," *Catholic Biblical Quarterly* 7 (1945): 377–97. For the use of Matthew in 1 Corinthians, see D. L. Dungan, *The Sayings of Jesus in the Churches of Paul* (Philadelphia: Fortress, 1971), 139–50.

during the first phase were portents that laid a foundation for the expansion of what was soon to follow:

1. The dispersion of the disciples during the persecution and martyrdom of Stephen, which first brought missionaries to Antioch (Acts 11), who converted a number of pagans in that wealthy city.
2. The conversion of Paul, God's chosen vessel for the conversion of the Gentiles, on the road to Damascus (Acts 9).
3. The reception of the centurion Cornelius and his family into the church by Peter with the approval of the Jerusalem church (Acts 10–11), without the obligation to be circumcised or to keep the food and marriage regulations that prevented Jews from associating with Gentiles.

Understandably, in the first phase the apostles were far too busy with the problems of the nascent church of Jerusalem to initiate a concerted drive to win over to Christ the Greek-speaking world of the Roman Empire; their immediate concern was quite properly their fellow Jews. However, the rapidly increasing numbers of converts at Antioch finally persuaded the Jerusalem apostles to send Barnabas there to investigate the new development, and he in turn invited Paul to join him in instructing these new followers of Jesus, who were soon to be labeled "Christians" by the general public. A severe famine in 45–46 led the Christians of Antioch to send Barnabas and Paul back to Jerusalem with a large sum to relieve the Christians' distress (Acts 11:25–30; 12:24–25). The Holy Spirit had intimated to Paul to use this opportunity to compare privately his teaching with that of the Twelve on the requirements of the church regarding the admission of Gentile converts. This was an urgent matter, as there was a powerful group of Pharisaic Christians in the mother church who wanted all converts to submit to the full rigor of the old law of Moses. Paul's meeting with Peter, James, and John is recorded in his letter to the Galatians (2:1–10),[7] and its outcome was a comprehensive understanding between him and the "pillars" (Paul's term), which included an agreement to observe their respective fields of ministry and a decision not to ask Gentile converts to take on the obligations of the Mosaic law.[8]

Shortly after Paul's return to Antioch, the Holy Spirit called him and Barnabas to set out on their first missionary journey to the districts of southern Galatia. Paul's astounding success (cf. Acts 14–15) quickly aroused the hostility of the strict Pharisees of Jerusalem, who sent a delegation to remonstrate with him. A fierce debate then took place in Antioch, and since neither side would bend, Paul had no option but to go up to Jerusalem and argue for the freedom of the Gentiles before the pillars (Acts 15:1–6). He was, of course, certain about the outcome, since previously they had already acknowledged his complete orthodoxy. The recognition of Gentile freedom from the law of Moses at the Council of Jerusalem in mid-century thus marked another milestone in the progress of the church (Acts 15:16–35).

During his third missionary journey Paul came to recognize the paramount need to integrate into one harmonious body the Jewish Christians with their Mosaic-Pharisaic traditions and the Greek and Roman converts. In his great letter to the Romans he had, in fact, already produced the necessary theological synthesis (Rom. 9–11). His missionary experience had proved that the Gospel of Matthew, which he was faithfully using as a follow-up to his oral

---

7. Cf. B. Orchard, "The Problem of Acts and Galatians," *Bulletin of the John Rylands Library* 28 (1944): 154–74.

8. See D. A. Black, "Weakness Language in Galatians," *Grace Theological Journal* 4 (1983): 15–36; idem, *Paul: Apostle of Weakness* (New York: Lang, 1984), 53–83.

teaching, did not answer all the questions of his Asian and Greek converts. This made him acutely aware of the need for a presentation of the Gospel nuanced to suit the mentality of the Hellenistic world.

He was now faced with a twofold task: (1) to produce a version of Matthew's Gospel that would meet the spiritual needs of the Greek world and (2) to make sure that this modified version would be acceptable to Peter and the other pillars. Before he came to the end of his third missionary journey Paul had chosen the man he needed for this difficult and delicate undertaking, his friend Luke, a physician, who joined him on the latter stages of his voyage back to Jerusalem. While there Paul found himself disenchanted by the reserved attitude of the elders who looked askance at what they regarded as the too easy terms on which Paul was admitting Greeks into the church. The Holy Spirit was now urging him to look toward Rome, and so he was longing to go there (Acts 19:21–22). As it so happened, Paul's hope did not materialize immediately because of his detention by the Romans for more than two years in their headquarters in Caesarea. Nevertheless, this enforced stay in Palestine turned out to be a blessing inasmuch as it provided Luke with sufficient time to check the details in Matthew's account of the life and ministry of Jesus, to interview many of those who had known him some thirty years before, and to prepare a new Gospel document closely modeled on Matthew's.

Through hindsight we can determine the assignment that Luke received from Paul by comparing the Gospels of Luke and Matthew and by noting Luke's deviations. In the first place, Luke carefully followed the main structure of Matthew throughout and generally adhered to the order of its various sections and anecdotes, though he also made highly interesting changes. For example, his story of the birth of Jesus is totally different from

Matthew's, which (as we have noted) was almost entirely apologetic in tone and content. Luke, however, provided a straightforward narrative that stems either directly or indirectly from Mary herself. When Luke came to Jesus' Galilean ministry he added certain details to each of the stories from Matthew's Gospel that he decided to adopt. Indeed, in one way or another he absorbed nearly everything that Matthew had written, and yet managed to add a good deal of extra material. Luke did this by omitting a number of duplicate stories (e.g., the famous Lukan omission of Matt. 14:22–16:12) and by inserting into the heart of the Matthean text at the end of the Galilean ministry (cf. Matt. 19:1–2) a section of no less than nine long chapters, Luke's central section (9:51–18:14), comprising (1) the excerpts that he had extracted from Matthew's six great discourses in order to lighten the content of his own version of them and (2) additional sayings and parables that Luke had collected. (It is perhaps worth noting here that Luke's central section roughly corresponds to the conjectural document known as Q, which many modern scholars consider to be one of the sources of Matthew and Luke.)

All the time he was composing, Luke kept his eye on the audience and readership for which Paul needed this Gospel, in particular on the Greeks' scientific bent, their desire to know names and dates and times, and their interest in the emancipation of women. Moreover, he made it his aim to reveal an aspect of Jesus that would impress the Gentile reader, namely by exhibiting him as a hero blessed by God, one too good for this world yet one who after his glorification was still bringing blessings to the world that he had rescued by his sacrificial death.

Luke completed his task in time to accompany Paul on the journey by sea to Rome, but there were two reasons for holding up the publication of his Gospel. In the first place, it was not a firsthand account since neither Luke nor Paul had been eyewitnesses of the ministry of Jesus, but was in the main a work of historical investigation; if it was to have credibility it would need the support of an eyewitness such as Peter. In the second place, and even more serious, was the possibility that the publication of this manifesto for Paul's Gentile converts would result in another eruption from the circumcision party, which was still active and was to remain so until the destruction of the temple in 70. Therefore, Luke's Gospel could not be published until this peril had been defused.

The Roman Phase (A.D. 62–67)

The situation was then as follows. The Gospel according to Matthew had been in circulation for some twenty years throughout the Christian world both inside and beyond the Roman Empire; and Paul was due to arrive in Rome as a prisoner of Caesar sometime in 61 or 62 (cf. Acts 28:30). Luke accompanied Paul, bringing with him a document that he compiled—in fact, a substantial adaptation of the Gospel of Matthew—during Paul's detention in Caesarea. Paul's former disciple Mark, however, who had left him earlier in his first missionary journey at Perga and had later gone with Barnabas to Cyprus, had since become Peter's devoted assistant (cf. 1 Peter 5:12–13). Nevertheless, the letters of Paul to the Colossians and to Philemon, traditionally said to have been written from Rome during Paul's detention (which ended not later than 63), reveal that he remained in intimate contact with both Mark and Luke (cf. Col. 4:10, 14; Philemon 24).

Paul was well aware of the importance attached by the secular Greek and Roman world to the testimony of actual eyewitnesses. But whereas the Gospel of Matthew had issued from the Jerusalem community, many of whom had known Jesus personally and could corroborate the witness of the Twelve preserved in that Gospel, neither Paul nor Luke had known Jesus while he walked on earth. Of course, Paul had been given a vision of the glorified

Christ, but he was still dependent on the Twelve for information about Jesus' earthly life.

As far as Luke was concerned, he too had to rely entirely on the tradition he had received from the apostles and from the Gospel of Matthew, to which he added his own personal researches into the events of the life of Jesus, gleaned from material supplied to him by many surviving witnesses whom he had succeeded in interrogating (cf. Luke 1:1–4). In order for Luke's work to be recognized as a true account and one worthy to be read in the Christian assembly either alongside or in place of Matthew's Gospel, Paul needed to have it endorsed by an apostolic eyewitness. Furthermore, although Paul's primary concern was to secure the publication of Luke's Gospel in the churches he himself had founded, he was also aware that once published it would inevitably find its way into the churches of the other apostles. Therefore, it was necessary for him well in advance to establish that Luke had not erred in any particular and to avoid any discourtesy to the apostles affected.

Peter happened to be in Rome at the time of Paul's captivity; and as he was the prime eyewitness of the public ministry of Jesus, Paul approached Peter to ask his advice about the best procedure. Peter realized that Paul needed the public assurance that Luke's book was in complete conformity with Peter's own recollections of Jesus, and he was happy to compare Luke's treatment with Matthew's parallel account of the events at which he himself had been a participant or had witnessed. Peter's plan was to give a series of speeches in the Roman location that he had designated for his weekly worship celebration. His secretary Mark helped prepare these talks, which were bound to excite the interest of the most influential Christians in Rome, including members of the Praetorium, which was the headquarters of the Roman army and the equivalent of our Pentagon. The news that Peter was going to give a series of lectures on the life of Jesus drew a great throng. Since it was the custom for public men to have their speeches recorded by shorthand writers, Mark arranged for shorthand writers of Greek to take down Peter's words just as he uttered them.[9]

On the appointed days, Peter, with Mark in attendance, went to the rostrum armed with the scroll of Matthew and the new scroll prepared by Luke. That these two Gospels were originally inscribed on scrolls and not on codices is certain because they are each just about the length of an ordinary commercial scroll, that is, about thirty feet in length. A scroll was typically written on only one side in narrow columns at right-angles to its length. When rolled up, it was tied with a cord and stored in one of a series of pigeon holes that constituted the bookcase of an educated man. To handle such a scroll required both hands, the right hand unrolling and the left rolling, until the reader arrived at the particular column he wanted to refer to.

Peter's intention was to refer only to those incidents in the life of Jesus of which he had been an eyewitness or could personally vouch for; therefore he would say nothing about the birth and resurrection narratives or about the collection of Jesus' sayings in Luke's central section. The simple fact that Peter was prepared to devote so much attention to this new work by Luke shows that he believed it to be worthy of adoption in its entirety by the church.

---

9. E. R. Richards shows in *The Secretary in the Letters of Paul* (Tübingen: Mohr/Siebeck, 1991), 26–29, that not only Latin but also Greek professional shorthand writers for *viva voce* verbatim recording were in regular employment in Rome at that time, so that Mark would have had no difficulty in getting Peter's words fully and accurately recorded, just as he uttered them. Cf. B. Orchard, "The Making and Publication of Mark's Gospel: An Historical Investigation," *Annales Theologici* 7 (1993): 369–93.

Peter, aided by Mark, divided for his own immediate purpose the Gospels of Matthew and Luke lying before him into five parts, that is, into five discourses *(didaskalias)* of twenty-five to forty minutes each, in the following manner:[10]

1. Beginning of ministry: Mark 1:2–3:19 = Matthew 3:1–5:1; Luke 3:1–6:19.
2. Early Galilean ministry: Mark 3:20–6:13 = Matthew 5:2–13:58; Luke 6:20–9:6.
3. Later Galilean ministry: Mark 6:14–10:1 = Matthew 14:1–18:35; Luke 9:7–50.
4. Post-Galilean ministry: Mark 10:2–13:37 = Matthew 19:1–25:46; Luke 9:51–21:38.
5. Passion narrative: Mark 14:1–16:8 = Matthew 26:1–28:20; Luke 22:1–24:53.

Further study of the text of Mark indicates that Peter delivered his recollections to his audience by word of mouth, checking with each gospel in turn as he went along. By conscious prearrangement his disciple and secretary Mark first handed him the scroll of Matthew and then at the appropriate point exchanged it for the scroll of Luke, thus alternately following the text of each Gospel, zigzagging, as it were, from one Gospel to the other.

Peter, of course, would have known the Gospel of Matthew almost, if not entirely, by heart, and therefore he tended to follow it more closely, but adding Luke's extra details wherever he could.

---

10. M. Hengel independently concluded that the Gospel of Mark was originally delivered in the Christian assembly in Rome and that the authority of Peter lies behind Mark's account; cf. his "Literary, Theological, and Historical Problems in the Gospel of Mark," in *The Gospel and the Gospels*, ed. P. Stuhlmacher (Grand Rapids: Eerdmans, 1983), 233–34.

He also adopted Luke's rearrangement of the early part of Matthew's Galilean ministry. Peter's treatment is also noteworthy for the introduction of so many vivid details that reveal him to be an eyewitness, such as Jesus' being asleep on the cushion in the stern of the boat (Mark 4:38) and the figure of two thousand swine who drowned themselves in the lake (Mark 5:13).

At the end of his fifth discourse Peter had covered all the main stories that Matthew and Luke had in common (except for the centurion's slave), from the baptism of John to Peter's personal discovery of the empty tomb. There, at the conclusion of the earthly ministry of Jesus, Peter ended his discourses, having exhausted his reminiscences, since Paul had his own personal visions of the risen Christ and did not require Peter's corroboration in this respect.

Those who had listened to Peter were delighted with everything they had heard, and they requested from Mark copies of what Peter had said. Tradition relates that when Peter was shown the transcript of his discourses he "exerted no pressure either to forbid it or to promote it" (Eusebius, *Ecclesiastical History* 6.14.7). In other words, Peter saw no particular advantage in promoting his own lectures, since Matthew had already made a complete Gospel available to his readers. In light of this public approbation, Paul was able to publish the text of Luke's Gospel in the churches of Achaia and Asia Minor without further delay or question.

It is thus clear that Peter was personally responsible for the text of our Gospel of Mark and that it was composed not only after Matthew and Luke, but also with their aid. However, despite its being highly prized by the church as the personal reminiscences of Peter, it did not enjoy universal circulation because it was not intended to supersede either Matthew or Luke. Indeed, it is rarely quoted by the early fathers, and the first commentary on it dates from only the fifth century. Its process of composition was quite unlike that of Matthew or Luke, and Peter had no intention of making it into a third Gospel.

How, then, does one explain how the last twelve verses (Mark 16:9–20), which describe the resurrection, were added to the Gospel? Some manuscripts record these verses, while others either omit them altogether or give a much shorter ending. The most plausible explanation is that after Mark had satisfied the immediate demand of those who wanted copies of the five discourses, which ended at Mark 16:8, the matter rested there until after the martyrdom of Peter and Mark's decision to go off to establish the church of Alexandria (67–69). As an act of piety to the memory of Peter, Mark then decided to publish an edition of the text that included the necessary sequel to the passion and death of Jesus. The attentive reader will observe that these verses form a summary catalogue of references to the resurrection stories of Matthew and Luke and were most likely added by Mark himself to round off the final discourse. But as the private edition of Mark, which lacked these verses, had already been in circulation for some years, the textual tradition has remained divided to this day.[11]

The Johannine Supplement

Christian tradition names John the son of Zebedee, the apostle and beloved disciple, as the fourth evangelist, and there is no solid reason to reject it. John wrote in Greek like the other evangelists and, in fact, knew all three Synoptic Gospels, making use especially of Luke. Although his final chapter (21) seems to be an afterthought, the manuscript tradition shows that the author published the Gospel as a whole. The date of publication, evidently from Ephesus, was possibly just before the death of John at the end of the century.

---

11. Cf. W. R. Farmer, *The Last Twelve Verses of Mark* (Cambridge: Cambridge University Press, 1974).

The purpose of John was to supplement in several ways the account about the ministry of Jesus provided by the Synoptic Gospels:

1. John thought it proper to set his Gospel in an eternal perspective by beginning with the heavenly existence of the Son of God (John 1:1–18).
2. While Matthew assumes Jesus to be the Messiah (Matt. 1:1), he does not explain that Jesus asserted his claim at the beginning of his ministry (the cleansing of the temple) because his plan was to place all the Jerusalem activities of Jesus in the last sections of his Gospel (Matt. 21–28). John makes it clear that Jesus staked his claim in categorical terms at the beginning (John 2).
3. John alone makes it clear that the public ministry of Jesus extended over two years (three Passovers) and possibly longer and that only part of it was spent in Galilee. The Galilean ministry was really an interlude forced upon Jesus by the hostility of the high priests. Nonetheless, John records that Jesus made some four visits to the Holy City to bring about the recognition of his messiahship before the final visit that resulted in his passion and death.
4. John alone records that during Jesus' visits to Jerusalem a number of intimate dialogues took place that uniquely reveal the mind and heart of Jesus and his relationship to his Father and to the Holy Spirit.

To sum up, it is John's intention to confirm and deepen the faith of his readers in Jesus as the consubstantial Son of God and thereby to ensure that by their faith they may obtain eternal life (20:30–31). The milieu of Johannine thought is clearly the world of Jewish thought, and not of Gnosticism with its timeless dualism of substance.[12] Nevertheless, the whole Gospel is permeated by a quiet but unmistakable polemic against Judaism, particularly against Jews who deny that Jesus is the Son of God and of heavenly origin.

Conclusion

No movement can be fully understood without knowledge of the community in which it originated. This applies to the Gospels just as much as to any other great movement that has permanently affected the world. Having this in view, we cannot simply regard the Gospels as a sudden and inexplicable outburst of genius. They are the fruit of a long process, initiated and determined by God and the calculated result of divine guidance.

Matthew is the fundamental Gospel and the most important, but each was written and published in response to a particular need of the church in a particular historical situation. The real significance of Mark lies in Peter's guarantee that Luke was fit to be read beside Matthew in the churches of both Peter and Paul. Mark is therefore to be viewed as the bridge between Matthew and Luke, that is, as a document enabling Luke's Gospel to be used freely in all the churches to which the authority of Peter, the chief eyewitness, extended; and it stands as a recognition of the equality of the Gentiles in all the churches.

We are also able to see why the church from a very early date, perhaps as early as the second century, placed Mark's Gospel between those of Matthew and Luke. By doing so, it signaled the church's acceptance of the tradition that the principal function of Mark was to introduce Luke to the Christian public and to confirm its equality with Matthew. The middle position of Mark had

---

12. See D. A. Black, "El Grupo de Juan: Helenismo y Gnosis," in *Origenes del Cristianismo*, ed. A. Piñero (Cordoba: el Almendro, 1991), 303–23.

nothing to do with the chronological order of the Gospels, for Luke was written before Mark's Gospel was even thought of; but its publication was delayed until its merits had been approved by Peter, who actually spoke the words that Mark recorded for him and for the church.

We may thus sum up the relationships between the Gospels as follows:

1. Matthew was composed to meet the urgent needs of the primitive church of Jerusalem (the church set up by Peter and the original apostles), which needed a manifesto defending its integrity and its right to exist in the earliest days.
2. Luke was written at the request of Paul to meet the urgent need of his churches to have their own manifesto to prove their full equality with Jewish Christians.
3. Mark was the result of the collaboration of Peter and Paul to make sure that the spiritual and doctrinal unity of the universal church was not impaired as a result of the appearance of Luke beside Matthew in the churches of both.
4. And John made it clear that the primary objective of Jesus throughout his public ministry was the winning over of the spiritual authorities in Jerusalem.

We must now inquire to what extent the above scenario reflects the historical evidence, including the judgment of the ecclesiastical writers of the first four centuries.

2

The Origins
of the Gospels

THE MOST ANCIENT TRADITION of the Christian church is that the fourfold Gospel came into existence in response to the needs experienced in some locality for an authoritative written word in addition to the continuous oral and unwritten preaching of the Gospel by the earliest apostles. The letters of Paul were also occasional writings, supplementary to his preaching and prompted by the particular needs of his converts. According to this same tradition, the twelve apostles were the sole original, authoritative, and inspired eyewitnesses of the words and deeds of Jesus. Furthermore, those teachings that they put into writing were also regarded by the churches that received them as having the same authority as their spoken words. And church tradition records that each of the four Gospels came into existence in response to the needs of the church at different moments during the lifetime of the original Twelve. This tradition is enshrined in the writings of the early fathers of the church and was generally adopted by all the churches, east and west, down to the eighteenth century.

The Enlightenment was the most powerful intellectual movement of the eighteenth century, and its avowed aim was to install human reason as the final arbiter in all human affairs in place of the Christian faith.[1] Its chief protagonists—Voltaire and Rousseau in France and Lessing and Reimarus in Germany—were determined to discredit the authority of the church in Protestant and Catholic countries not only on account of their support of the corrupt political system, but also for relying on the authenticity of the Gospels, which they claimed could not have been written by the apostles. These philosophers maintained that the earliest incontrovertible written evidence for the authenticity of the Gospels dated from nearly a hundred years after the death of the apostles and that therefore the Gospels themselves must be based on legend and hearsay created during this period. And though these arguments have since been refuted, skepticism about the value of that same tradition still exists in the university faculties in Europe and America. There also remains in some minds the opinion that to be a "believer" is to be handicapped in the pursuit of the truth. We shall have to disregard such theological impediments for the present and move on to scientifically examine the three independent lines of argument for evaluating the authenticity of the Gospels. The first of these is to set out afresh the main lines of the external evidence and to evaluate it in light of modern research. The second line is the internal comparison of the Gospel texts to discover their sources and their interconnections. And the third is to show that no emergent hypothesis is credible unless it is viable in light of the known history of the church and the Roman Empire at that time.

Before setting out the external evidence for the Gospels, it is

---

1. For a summary of the origins of the Enlightenment, including its divorce of reason both from the tradition of faith and from tradition in principle, see "The Enlightenment" in *The Oxford Dictionary of the Christian Church*, ed. F. L. Cross (3d ed.; Oxford: Oxford University Press, 1997), 546–47.

in order to remind the reader that the ancient churchmen were primarily interested in the spiritual authority of the Gospels, that is, in their being the actual witnesses of the apostles or a witness sanctioned by the apostles. Only when church tradition came to be seriously questioned and challenged by heretics and dissidents did Christian writers bestir themselves to defend it vigorously. Hence, the records of the provenance of the Gospels are sparse until Marcion in the middle of the second century decided to discard all of the Gospels except his expurgated version of Luke. This is why the most important information about Mark emerged in response to critical challenges only in the years 150–250. During this period church apologists condemned the proliferation of apocryphal Gospels, affirmed the apostolicity of the four canonical Gospels, and gathered the information about their origins that Eusebius was to preserve and systematize in the fourth century.

These fathers were aware of but not, it seems, interested in the question of the mutual dependence of the Gospels. That is, the first Christians simply asked for assurance that the Gospels were truly the inspired reminiscences of the apostles. The question is: Were the fathers in a position to give this assurance?

The Principal Patristic Witnesses

Here, then, beginning with Justin, are the chief recorded witnesses of the first four centuries, presented in chronological sequence according to the date of the documents in which they first appear.[2]

1. Justin (ca. 100–165; *Dialogue with Trypho* 106.9–10): "And when it is said that he [Jesus] changed the name of one of his

---

2. I have freshly translated these texts taken primarily from the Loeb Classical Library (Harvard University Press).

apostles to Peter, and when it is written in his [Peter's] memoirs that this happened. . ."

2. Irenaeus (ca. 130–200; *Against Heresies* 3.1.1–2; cf. Eusebius, *Ecclesiastical History* 5.8.1–4, whose Greek is given in brackets): "So Matthew brought out a written gospel among the Jews in their own style [*tē idia autōn dialektō*], when Peter and Paul were preaching the gospel at Rome and founding the church. But after their demise Mark himself, the disciple and recorder [*hermēneutēs*] of Peter, has also handed on to us in writing what had been proclaimed by Peter. And Luke, the follower of Paul, set forth in a book the gospel that was proclaimed by him. Later John, the disciple of the Lord and the one who leaned against his chest, also put out a gospel while residing in Ephesus of Asia."

3. Clement of Alexandria (ca. 150–215; *Adumbrationes in epistolas canonicas* on 1 Peter 5:13): "Mark, the follower of Peter, while Peter was publicly preaching the gospel at Rome in the presence of some of Caesar's knights and uttering many testimonies about Christ, on their asking him to let them have a record of the things that had been said, wrote the gospel that is called the Gospel of Mark from the things said by Peter, just as Luke is recognized as the pen that wrote the Acts of the Apostles and as the translator of the Letter of Paul to the Hebrews."

4. Tertullian (ca. 160–225; *Against Marcion* 4.2.1–2): "I lay it down to begin with that the documents of the gospel have the apostles for their authors, and that this task of promulgating the gospel was imposed upon them by the Lord himself. . . . In short, from among the apostles, John and Matthew implant in us the faith, while from among the apostolic men Luke and Mark reaffirm it."

5. Origen (ca. 185–254; *Homilies on Luke* 1): "For Matthew did

not 'take in hand' but wrote by the Holy Spirit, and so did Mark and John and also equally Luke. . . . For there is also the gospel 'according to Thomas,' and that 'according to Matthias,' and many others. These are the ones 'that have been taken in hand.' But the church of God accepts only the four."

6. Muratorian Fragment (second century): "At which, however, he [Mark] was present and has thus stated. In the third place, the book of the Gospel according to Luke. . . The fourth of the Gospels is John's, one of the disciples."

7. Anti-Marcionite Prologue to Luke (second century): "There were already gospels in existence, that according to Matthew, written down in Judea, and that according to Mark in Italy. But guided by the Holy Spirit, he [Luke] composed in the regions around Achaia the whole of the gospel."

8. Old Latin Prologue to Mark (recension 2; second century): "Mark, who was also called Stubfinger because he had shorter fingers with regard to the other dimensions of the body. He had been the disciple and recorder *[interpres]* of Peter, whom he followed, just as he had heard him relating. Having been asked by the brethren in Rome, he wrote this short gospel in the regions of Italy. When Peter heard about it, he approved and authorized it to be read to the church with [his own] authority. But after the demise of Peter, taking this gospel that he had composed he journeyed to Egypt, and being ordained the first bishop of Alexandria he founded the church there, preaching Christ. He was a man of such great learning and austerity of life that he induced all the followers of Christ to imitate his example. Last of all John, perceiving that the external facts had been made plain in the gospel, and being urged by his friends and inspired by the Spirit, composed a spiritual gospel."

9. Eusebius (ca. 260–340; *Ecclesiastical History* 2.15.1–16.1): "And thus when the Divine Word had made its home among them, the power of Simon was quenched and immediately destroyed, together with the man himself. To such a degree did the flame of true piety illuminate the minds of Peter's hearers that, not being satisfied with having just one hearing or with the unwritten teaching of the divine proclamation, with every sort of entreaty they urged Mark, whose gospel it is reputed to be, being the follower of Peter, to bequeath to them also in writing the record of the teaching handed on to them by word [of mouth], nor did they let up before convincing the man. And by this means they became the cause of the gospel writing that is said to be 'according to Mark.' They also say that when the apostle learned what had happened, the Spirit having revealed this to him, he was pleased with the enthusiasm of the men and authorized the writing for reading in the churches. Clement in the sixth book of *The Outlines* relates the story, and the bishop of Hierapolis, Papias by name, bears joint witness to him. He also says that Peter mentions Mark in his First Letter, and that he composed this in Rome itself, which they say that he himself indicates, speaking figuratively of the city of Babylon, by these words: 'The Elect [Lady] in Babylon greets you, along with Mark my son.' Now they say that this Mark was the first to be sent to Egypt to preach the gospel that he had also committed to writing, and was the first to establish churches in Alexandria itself."

10. Bishop Papias of Hierapolis (ca. 60–130; quoted in Eusebius, *Ecclesiastical History* 3.39.15–16): "This too the Elder [*ho presbyteros*] used to say: Mark, having become the recorder [*hermēneutēs*] of Peter, indeed wrote accurately albeit not in order whatever he [Peter] remembered of the things either said or done by the Lord. For he had neither heard the Lord

nor was a follower of him, but later, as I said, of Peter, who used to deliver his teachings *[didaskalias]* in the form of short stories *[chreias]*, but not making as it were a literary composition of the Lord's sayings, so that Mark did not err at all when he wrote down certain things just as he [Peter] recalled them. For he had but one intention: not to leave out anything he had heard nor to falsify anything in them. This is what was related by Papias about Mark's [Gospel]. But about Matthew's this was said: So then Matthew composed the sayings *[ta logia]* in a Hebrew style *[hebraidi dialektō]*, and each recorded them as he was able."

11. Clement of Alexandria (ca. 150–215; quoted in Eusebius, *Ecclesiastical History* 6.14.5–7): "And again in the same books [*The Outlines*] Clement has set down a tradition of the earliest elders about the order of the Gospels, and it has this form. He used to say that the earliest written gospels were those containing the genealogies, and that the Gospel of Mark had this arrangement. When Peter had publicly preached the word in Rome and by the Spirit had proclaimed the gospel, those present, who were numerous, urged Mark, as one who had followed him for a long time and remembered what had been spoken, to record what was said. And he did this, handing over the gospel to those who had asked for it. And when Peter got to know about it, he exerted no pressure either to forbid it or to promote it."

12. Origen (ca. 185–254; quoted in Eusebius, *Ecclesiastical History* 6.25.3–6): "[Origen] testifies that he knows only four gospels. . . . The first written was that according to the one-time tax collector but later apostle of Jesus Christ, Matthew, who published it for the believers from Judaism, composed in Hebrew characters *[grammasin hebraikois]*. And second, that according to Mark, composed as Peter guided. . . . And third,

that according to Luke, the gospel praised by Paul, composed for those from the Gentiles. After them all, that according to John."

13. Jerome (ca. 345–420; *Epistle* 120.11): "[Paul] had Titus as a recorder *[interpres]*, just as blessed Peter had Mark, whose gospel consists of Peter's narration and the latter's writing."

14. Augustine (ca. 354–430; *De consensu evangelistarum* 1.3–4): "Therefore these four evangelists, well known to the whole world, four in number, perhaps because of the four parts of the world, are said to have been written in this order: first Matthew, then Mark, third Luke, last John. . . . Of the four, Matthew alone is said to have been written in Hebrew. . . . Mark seems to have followed him as his footman and abbreviator."

Evaluation of the Patristic Witnesses

Let us first make some general observations about the quality of these texts.[3]

1. They have been preserved from the earliest times because they are the witnesses of the most distinguished churchmen of those days, men whose integrity and competence were universally recognized.

2. These witnesses represent the widest possible distribution: Irenaeus of Lyons who originally came from Asia Minor; Clement and Origen who came from Egypt; Eusebius and Jerome from Palestine; Augustine from North Africa; while the prologues represent the consensus of a number of European churches.

---

3. A fuller treatment of these citations will be found in B. Orchard and H. Riley, *The Order of the Synoptics* (Macon, Ga.: Mercer University Press, 1987), part 2.

3. Whenever the four Gospels are mentioned, Matthew always heads the list.

4. As for "the sayings" *(ta logia)* of Papias, Eusebius assumes that Papias is referring to the Gospel of Matthew that we all know, and not to a "proto-Matthew" or a collection of sayings such as Q is reputed to be.[4] For Papias, and for Eusebius, "Matthew" is of course the apostle, and Papias's description of his Gospel as "the Lord's sayings" is particularly apt in light of the discourses of Jesus so characteristic of Matthew. However, even though *ta logia* describes the Gospel of Matthew by means of its content (for it is par excellence a compilation of the sayings of Jesus), the absence of any explanatory definition of the expression excludes the possibility of Papias having meant that Matthew *limited* his account to sayings. Indeed, the use of *logia* in the sense of "oracles" (i.e., inspired Scriptures) is quite common in early Christian times (cf. Rom 3:2, where *ta logia tou theou* refers to the entire Old Testament).

5. The gospel named after Luke is attributed to Luke, the disciple of Paul, by all authorities.

6. Our sources clearly reveal some problem with regard to the origin of Mark. When all four Gospels are mentioned, Mark as a rule is given second place, but the important tradition recorded by Clement of Alexandria relates that both Matthew and Luke came into existence before Mark. There are two questions here. First, is it possible for Mark to be regarded from two different aspects as both the second and the third—third perhaps in order of actual composition, but second in order of authority as the work of Peter? Second, can we discover exactly what the various authorities meant by saying

---

4. See W. G. Kümmel, *Introduction to the New Testament* (Nashville: Abingdon, 1965), 43–44, who concurs that *ta logia* refers to our Gospel of Matthew.

that Mark "wrote" a gospel? The almost invariable use by the fathers of the word *hermēneutēs* (Latin *interpres*) to describe Mark's function proclaims that he was not the author in the normal sense, but rather the "go-between" or "interpreter" of Peter.[5] Jerome has neatly seized upon this in his phrase that Mark's Gospel was "Peter's narration and Mark's writing." Papias, too, explains Mark's function as that of a "go-between" or "recorder."

Let us now sum up the positive information contained about the Gospels in these texts and then see if it is possible to meet the criticism of the skeptics. According to tradition, Matthew is the first written Gospel and John is the last. Luke was sponsored by Paul and is usually placed third. The problem lies with the origins of Mark. The tradition gives the following information about the composition of Mark; we may state them and assess their value.

1. Peter is in all cases described as the person responsible for creating the text of Mark (in Greek of course), which is nothing other than Peter's "memoirs" (Justin).
2. Peter did not write down his Gospel stories; he spoke them aloud to an audience.
3. Mark his disciple retrieved what Peter had spoken and did so at the request of Peter's enthusiastic audience.
4. The "Elder" of *Ecclesiastical History* 3.39, if not the apostle

---

5. The term *hermēneutēs* signifies someone who passes on the message received from another without alteration or modification, that is, a "go-between" or "recorder." In its original sense it cannot mean an editor or one who "interprets" in the sense of explaining someone's message to someone else. Applied to Mark, it means that he was no more than the instrument of communication between Peter and his audience. See H. G. Liddell and R. Scott, *A Greek-English Lexicon*, rev. H. S. Jones (Oxford: Clarendon, 1996), 690.

John himself then at least a figure contemporary with and of the same stature as John,[6] authoritatively stated that Mark as Peter's *hermēneutēs* was able to reproduce exactly what Peter had said. This is an apparent reference to the reaction of some contemporary critics of the Gospel of Mark to certain of Peter's recorded statements, but the Elder was able to assure them that Mark had not altered anything at all but had faithfully recorded exactly what Peter had said.

5. The content of what Peter had spoken consisted of testimonies regarding what the Lord had "said and done" in the form of short stories *(chreiai)*, the very kind of literary form that makes up the bulk of Mark.[7]

6. Clement of Alexandria gives some idea of the occasion of Peter's talks when he says that they took place in Rome before an audience of "Caesar's knights"—members of the Roman Praetorium—and therefore an audience containing a number of high government officials.

---

6. J. H. Chapman, *John the Presbyter* (Oxford: Oxford University Press, 1911), 41–48, points out that the most likely identification of Papias's *presbyteros* is John the apostle and disciple of the Lord, universally known as the Elder (2–3 John); cf. Orchard and Riley, *Order of the Synoptics*, 177–84. It is disingenuous for critics to profess complete ignorance regarding the identity of this Elder; the apostle John is in any case the most likely and most obvious candidate.

7. J. Kürzinger is undoubtedly correct in understanding *chreia* as the contemporary grammatical term for a special kind of anecdote with a striking conclusion; see *Papias von Hierapolis und die Evangelien des Neuen Testaments* (Regensburg: Pustet, 1983), chap. 3 n. 8. Kürzinger gives a number of examples to show that the term *chreia* was commonly used in this period to describe the literary form of the kind of story units we find in Mark. Cf. R. O. P. Taylor, *The Groundwork of the Gospels* (Oxford: Oxford University Press, 1946), 76: "It may be remarked, at this point, that the definition [of *chreia*] fits the detachable little stories, of which so much of Mark consists."

7. Clement also connects this Gospel of Mark with the two other Synoptic Gospels when he states that it was subsequent to those "containing the genealogies."[8]

8. There is, however, a parallel tradition in Irenaeus, seemingly supported by the Muratorian Canon and most other authorities, that Mark was second after Matthew, and Luke third.

9. Jerome, as we have seen, understood the above evidence as proving the Gospel of Mark to be "Peter's narration and Mark's writing."

10. There is no hint that Matthew ever occupied any other position than that of first in the minds of the early fathers. Moreover, the only passage that suggests that Luke and Mark were composed "after the demise of Peter" is the result of a misapprehension and cannot be sustained (see below).

11. The chronological order Matthew–Luke–Mark is, in fact, what one would naturally expect, seeing that Christianity spread from Jerusalem into Asia Minor and Greece and thence westward to Rome and the west.

In conclusion, the patristic and historical evidence shows that all three Synoptic Gospels appeared in the lifetimes of the apostles

---

8. In his article, "Clement of Alexandria on the 'Order' of the Gospels," *New Testament Studies* 47, no. 1 (2001): 118-125, Stephen C. Carlson argues that Clement was referring, not to Matthew and Luke being "written *beforehand*," but rather to their being "written/published *publicly*." Carlson concludes that Clement's statement can no longer be used to support Markan posteriority to Matthew and Luke. However, although the rendering "publish publicly" is possible for the verb *prographo*, Carlson's conclusion that "the gospels with the genealogies were written before the public, as gospels for all Christians" (125) does nothing to diminish the Fourfold Gospel Hypothesis. Indeed, the "public" nature of Matthew and Luke comports well with the fathers' assertion that Mark was published for a limited audience only.

Peter and Paul, the twin founders of the western church, and also devotes much space to explaining how Mark came to exist. This, of course, suits perfectly the Fourfold-Gospel Hypothesis but utterly fails to support the priority of Mark at any point, since the latter hypothesis generally requires all three Gospels to have been published after the death of Peter around 66/67. How do Markan priorists deal with this evidence?

An Evaluation of Markan Priority

The patristic evidence for the authenticity and historicity of the Gospels is not normally discussed nowadays at any length, if at all, by Markan priorists. Today the academic guild, both in Europe and North America, assumes that the patristic evidence is basically legendary and unreliable. The reasons most often given are the following:[9]

1. The patristic testimony is said to be inconsistent, contradictory, and insecurely based.
2. It is highly unlikely that an eyewitness authority like Peter (if Peter is behind Mark) would have wanted to produce a document dependent on Matthew and Luke if, in fact, these two Gospels were already in existence. And why, in this case, did Mark leave out so much?
3. Internal evidence is said to be decisive for Markan priority.

As to #1, since the agreement of the fathers on the priority of Matthew is too strong to be denied, this testimony is devaluated by (a) disparaging their authority, (b) accusing them of copying one another mechanically, the earliest attestations being said to be doubtful or obscure, (c) implying that they did not know the

---

9. The following discussion is indebted to B. Orchard, *The Two-Gospel Hypothesis* (London: Ealing Abbey, 1989), 7–20.

actual facts, or (d) asserting that they did not understand author-ship as we understand it today.

The first three objections need no refutation when we recall the scholarship, intelligence, and integrity of these outstanding churchmen.[10] It is interesting to note that classical Greek and Roman scholars have never shared modern biblical critics' distrust of ancient ecclesiastical writers regarding the authority and au-thenticity of the Gospels. They have always been willing to give them at least as much credence as they have given to the secular historians of antiquity and to recognize that the skills of ancient scholars in critical analysis were just as sharp as those of modern critics, even though they worked with less sophisticated tools.[11]

---

10. We know, for instance, that Clement of Alexandria (died ca. 215) took the trouble to sift evidence from all over the Roman Empire and beyond (cf. Eusebius, *Ecclesiastical History* 5.11). Furthermore, the main witnesses are the greatest scholars of the period 150–250, who could not all have been deceived, and there was continuous spiritual and intellectual exchange at all levels between the churches from the ear-liest days. It would be a slur on the integrity and learning of the fa-thers to argue that their unanimity was the result of simply repeating one another in parrotlike fashion in each succeeding generation.

11. There are some hopeful signs that a better appreciation of the ma-turity of ancient scholarship is now on the way. Cf. E. G. Turner, *Greek Papyri* (Oxford: Clarendon, 1980), 99: "We can now see that the higher critics of the nineteenth century underrated the value of ancient learning, and therefore at times took a cavalier attitude to the statements of ancient scholars." See also A. N. Sherwin-White, *Roman Society and Roman Law in the New Testament* (Oxford: Ox-ford University Press, 1963), 186–93, esp. 187: "It is astonishing that while Graeco-Roman historians have been growing in confidence, the twentieth-century study of the gospel narratives, starting from no less promising material, has taken so gloomy a turn in the de-velopment of form-criticism that the more advanced exponents of it apparently maintain—so far as an amateur can understand the matter—that the historical Christ is unknowable and the history of his mission cannot be written."

With regard to the assertion that the church fathers did not understand authorship as we understand it today, the ecclesiastical tradition never claimed that the evangelists were creative "authors" in the strict sense, but only that their writings belonged to the category of personal recollections. They are simply personal reminiscences put into convenient shape for the benefit of the churches for which they were written. The external evidence is consistent that Matthew is the work of that apostle and that Mark and Luke were sponsored and authorized by Peter and Paul. Since this tradition was never questioned it must have been in existence from the very beginning, even though the earliest surviving written records mentioning them by name date only from the heresy of Marcion (mid-second century), which caused the fathers to promulgate these traditions explicitly in their apologetic writings. Indeed, it is the modern critics, blinded by their conviction of the priority of Mark, who have failed to accept the obvious message of the patristic evidence. That is why they have misunderstood the significance of the texts that always describe the disciple Mark as the go-between or agent of Peter and never as the author; yet the critics ignore this and make him out to be a writer who remembers what Peter said and not simply the agent for the recording of Peter's lectures. Again, it is often claimed that Irenaeus asserted that Mark wrote after the death of Peter, when he asserted nothing of the kind.[12] Furthermore, many have

---

12. Many contemporary scholars claim that Irenaeus (*Against Heresies* 3.1.1) was here intending to date Mark after the death of Peter and Paul. If this were the correct interpretation, then it would contradict the other patristic witnesses, who all assert or imply that Mark heard and recorded Peter during his lifetime. Such a superficial reading is, however, a serious misinterpretation of Irenaeus, whose point is solely to emphasize the contemporary authority of Mark, whose gospel has faithfully preserved and "handed on" the authentic preaching of Peter.

overlooked J. Kürzinger's discovery that *hebraidi dialektō* almost certainly means "in a Hebrew style," and not "in (the) Hebrew language."[13] Thus, in light of the most recent research, the main patristic texts down to Jerome are never contradictory and are perfectly clear in all essentials; the one or two secondary inconsistencies can easily bear a consistent interpretation.

As to #2, the critics argue that if both Matthew and Luke were in existence it would be absurd for an eyewitness like Peter to submit himself to these documents. But the critics forget that if Matthew alone was in existence and Paul wanted to circulate a document like Luke's Gospel, then there would at once be excellent grounds for asking Peter to step in and give his approval from his own eyewitness experience to this new Gospel of Luke. And this is, in fact, our thesis, with Mark acting as Peter's *hermēneutēs*.

Adherents of Markan priority often pose the question, "Why should anyone have wanted to write a new gospel that omitted so

---

13. J. Kürzinger, "Das Papiaszeugnis und die Erstgestalt des Matthäusevangeliums," *Biblische Zeitschrift* 4 (1960): 19–38; idem, "Irenäus und sein Zeugnis zur Sprache des Matthäusevangeliums," *New Testament Studies* 10 (1963): 108–15. Kürzinger explains that in the first century *dialektos* commonly meant both "language" and "style," so that the phrase in *Ecclesiastical History* 3.39.16 could mean either "in a Hebrew language" or "in a Hebrew style," depending on context. In the present context, the Elder had been explaining some problems in the style and/or content of Mark, since it possessed neither the Jewish style of Matthew nor the normal literary style of a Greek biography such as Luke's. The absence of the definite article in the phrase *hebraidi dialektō* is further support of the view taken here. Cf. Orchard and Riley, *Order of the Synoptics,* 198–99 (= excursus 2: "The Origin of the Notion of an 'Aramaic' Gospel of Matthew"). Origen, mistakenly thinking that Papias was referring to the language in which Matthew was written, stated that Matthew was "composed in Hebrew characters." This error was perpetuated by later writers.

much from his sources?"[14] The fundamental flaw in this argument is precisely the baseless assumption that Mark (or Peter) intended to write a Gospel like the other two. Mark is quite a different kind of document. The Fourfold-Gospel Hypothesis, in fact, asserts that Mark's account of the life of Jesus was never intended to be a rival Gospel. Mark is not a book in the sense in which the ancient Greeks and Romans understood the term; it is simply the spoken word directly captured and set down on paper exactly as it was originally uttered. It consists of a long chain of *chreiai* (short stories) about a heroic personage, recorded in a nonliterary style and without any formal beginning or ending. The above question concerning Markan omissions is therefore totally irrelevant, because Mark is not to be reckoned a Gospel in the sense that Matthew and Luke truly are.

As to #3, because it has long been popular to devalue the patristic evidence and the ecclesiastical background of the Gospels that we have just been examining, modern students of the synoptic problem prefer to devote their attention to attempts to solve it solely through the study of the internal evidence. But far from achieving their objective in this way, the result of over two hundred years of endeavor has been frustration and stalemate,

---

14. Cf. E. P. Sanders and M. Davies, *Studying the Synoptic Gospels* (London: SCM, 1989), 92: "The strongest arguments against the Griesbach hypothesis are general, not technical. Why would anyone write a shorter version of Matthew and Luke, carefully combining them, and leaving out so much—such as the Lord's prayer and the beatitudes—while gaining nothing except perhaps room for such trivial additions as the duplicate phrases and minor details . . . ?" This considerably mollifies B. H. Streeter's famous statement in *The Four Gospels* (New York: Macmillan, 1924), 158: "Only a lunatic would leave out Matthew's account of the Infancy, the Sermon on the Mount, and practically all the parables, in order to get room for purely verbal expansion of what was retained."

and not a few critics have come to the conclusion that the problem is insoluble—and so it is, without the two other criteria. For internal criticism deals with anonymous and unidentifiable editors and sources and never comes down to flesh-and-blood realities, to known persons and situations. Yet, as we have seen, the Gospels came into existence in particular times and places, as the brainchildren of particular individuals under certain given pressures, and for that reason were highly revered and sought after. All that internal literary criticism can do is show how an existing text *could* have originated in more than one way. But the decision as to which is the *correct* way requires the help of history, if it is to be reached at all. Thus there is more than one way of envisaging the creation of the text, even though one way may seem more probable than the other. In our view, the source theory that best reflects the actual historical circumstances is most likely to be the true explanation.

The Fourfold-Gospel Hypothesis needs no hypothetical documents to support it, nor any restrictions. It holds that the second evangelist knew the first and that the third knew the other two, and it has practically the total support of the patristic and historical evidence. And while the Fourfold-Gospel Hypothesis can easily be made to fit all the evidence, critical and patristic, the same cannot be said of the Markan priority hypothesis.[15] The latter is built upon a deliberate and *a priori* rejection of the ancient patristic evidence and the denial of any suggestion of a direct connection between the apostles and the Gospel writings. In short, the Markan

---

15. Thus, for example, if Clement's assertion that the earliest Gospels were those containing the genealogies is allowed to stand, then it destroys the last vestige of external support for the priority of Mark in addition to providing strong external support for the Fourfold-Gospel Hypothesis. All objections to Clement's statement founder on the fact that Eusebius accepted it as authentic.

priority hypothesis is based on a number of dubious assumptions, for example, that things are not as the fathers perceived them; that Matthew and Luke are, despite appearances, secondary to Mark; and that the hypothetical source Q was a vitally important document in the first fifty years after the resurrection but was lost through shocking carelessness.[16]

Since, therefore, according to the rules of interpretation laid down in the Enlightenment tradition, it is considered unscientific to give credence to the patristic testimony that the apostle Matthew was the author of the Gospel that bears his name, the exegetes of this tradition have a compelling need to find another way of explaining how the Gospels came to be composed. Unable to allow the unity of authorship imposed by the mind and skill of an eyewitness apostle, they naturally tend to see Matthew as an amalgam of different sources, consisting partly of genuine material from the apostle (but without agreement as to which is apostolic and which is not) and partly of material from several sources—a birth narrative source, a John the Baptist source, a parables source, a passion narrative source, a resurrection source—and various other form-critical divisions that seem to reflect their conjectures regarding the needs and tensions of the primitive church.

To bring all this material into coherent order, Markan priorists invoke final editors of two sources in particular: the editor of Mark (or a recension of it) and the independent editor of a contemporary sayings source Q. Mark is therefore seen as the source of all

---

16. See E. E. Ellis, "Gospels Criticism: A Perspective on the State of the Art," in *The Gospel and the Gospels*, ed. P. Stuhlmacher (Grand Rapids: Eerdmans, 1991), 33–37. On the status of Q in current Gospel studies, see D. L. Bock, "Questions about Q," in *Rethinking the Synoptic Problem*, ed. D. R. Beck and D. A. Black (Grand Rapids: Baker, 2001), 41–64.

the material that Matthew has in common with it, while Q is said to be the source of all the material common to Matthew and Luke alone, that is, material not found in Mark. In addition, both Matthew and Luke have some special sources. All this material is said to have been revised by the final editor of Matthew independently of the final editor of Luke, for the notion of two editors working in parallel, yet not knowing what the other is doing, is normally a further condition of Markan priority.

Since the creation of our Greek Matthew is usually assumed to have taken place during the years 70–90 (often called the "tunnel period" because we have no definite knowledge of what took place during it), the champions of Markan priority have to envisage and/or create a hypothetical Judeo-Christian community situated somewhere between Damascus and Antioch, one that somehow retained some vestiges of the Jewish way of life destroyed in 70. It is arbitrarily postulated that a period of between fifty and sixty years after the resurrection would give enough time for these various sources to mature and for some skillful editor to be able to combine them into our present Greek Matthew and to present them to his own local church. But there still remain for this hypothesis two further problems: the problem of very rapidly getting this document accepted by the Christian churches everywhere, and the problem of why it was expressly attributed to the apostle Matthew when it clearly had very little to do with him. For there is no ancient evidence whatever to show that in the mainstream churches there was any need for pseudepigraphic attribution, although it was a favorite device among the fringe and heretical churches of the period.[17] The mainstream churches had presumably already happily accepted the Gospel of Mark, a

---

17. Cf. T. L. Wilder, "Pseudonymity and the New Testament," in *Interpreting the New Testament*, ed. D. A. Black and D. S. Dockery (Nashville: Broadman & Holman, 2001), 293–332.

secondary personage of no great authority compared with Peter and Paul. So why should this work, supposedly based on Mark, need to be falsely bolstered by attribution to the apostle Matthew?[18] It is asking too much to require us to believe that the mainstream churches could have been totally deceived or could have permitted such a deception on so important a matter; too many people would have been "in the know" for any group or any church to have been able to foist such an apocryphal Gospel on the church at large in total silence.[19]

These general flaws in the Markan priority hypothesis should in themselves be enough to discredit it entirely. But as they have not done so, it is necessary to ask the further question: Has this hypothesis been successful in proving the priority of Mark over Matthew and Luke when it comes to comparing particular texts? The only truthful answer is that it has not. Of course, if the critic begins by accepting the background and the presuppositions created on behalf of this hypothesis, then it is possible to see it

---

18. Explanations for this phenomenon include the suggestion of M. G. Reddish, *An Introduction to the Gospels* (Nashville: Abingdon, 1997), 38, that the name Matthew was chosen instead of another because of the similarity between his name and the Greek word for "disciple" *(mathētēs)*. Such explanations are recourses of desperation.

19. Recently E. E. Ellis, "The Synoptic Gospels and History," in *Authenticating the Activities of Jesus,* ed. B. Chilton and C. A. Evans (Leiden: Brill, 1999), 53–56, notes how the discoveries at Qumran and a greater appreciation for the literacy of first-century Jews have countered the attempt to compare oral transmission to that of other later, less literate, folk culture. He also notes that Jewish tradition was passed on with great care and that the presence of eyewitnesses served as a check on any fluidity in the tradition. He further emphasizes that putting key events down in writing would not have required a long passage of time and that the basic outlines of the chronological/geographical flow of Jesus' ministry would have been remembered accurately.

offering a seemingly satisfactory explanation of the literary phenomena, provided that one can forget the rest of the evidence. There are, however, four literary phenomena still needing explanation when a comparison of the Synoptic texts is undertaken:

1. The pericope order and the zigzag phenomenon.
2. The extra detail of Mark.
3. The minor agreements between Matthew and Luke against Mark.
4. Markan conflation of Matthew and Luke.

First, J. J. Griesbach concluded that the zigzag phenomenon showed Markan dependence on Matthew and Luke:

> Briefly, you can see with your own eyes, Mark having the volumes of Matthew and Luke at hand, continually consulting each, extracting from each whatever he thought would most benefit his readers, now laying aside Matthew, now Luke for a little, but always returning to the very same place of either one where he had begun to diverge from him.[20]

Griesbach provided a table to show how Mark hops from one to the other. This statement has been used by some to disparage Griesbach, but it is a fact that demands explanation. The incorporation of such a phenomenon would be absurd if the author of Mark was really writing a book; but if he was not, then there is a perfectly reasonable explanation for it, as we have seen.

Second, the fact that the style of Mark (i.e., his rough language and vivid detail) is colloquial and nonliterary in no way argues that

---

20. B. Orchard and T. R. W. Longstaff (eds.), *J. J. Griesbach: Synoptic and Text-Critical Studies, 1776–1976* (Cambridge: Cambridge University Press, 1978), 108.

Mark was early but only that the Gospel's language and diction reflect the author's purposes in writing.[21] The vivid detail that Mark often adds to the stories of Matthew and Luke suggests an eyewitness who knew both of the other Gospels. Furthermore, extra detail is more often than not a sign of lateness and dependence.[22]

Third, the so-called minor agreements of Matthew and Luke against Mark are generally allowed to weigh heavily in favor of the Fourfold-Gospel Hypothesis, for they are *prima facie* evidence for literary contact between Matthew and Luke. Modern supporters of Markan priority have no solid answer to the question: How can it be explained that in some 180 cases Matthew and Luke, independently and without knowledge of each other, joined in leaving out identical phrases and sentences from the Gospel of Mark if this had been their source?[23]

Finally, there are various literary signs that Mark has conflated Matthew and Luke. An abundance of examples can be given.[24] The same conclusion is suggested by Mark's short annotations, corresponding to the footnotes that appear in modern books.

Given the provisos that always accompany the Markan priority

---

21. See D. A. Black, "Some Dissenting Notes on R. Stein's *The Synoptic Problem* and Markan 'Errors,'" *Filología Neotestamentaria* 1 (1988): 95–101; idem, "Discourse Analysis, Synoptic Criticism, and the Problem of Markan Grammar: Some Methodological Considerations," in *Linguistics and New Testament Interpretation*, ed. D. A. Black (Nashville: Broadman & Holman, 1992), 89–98.

22. T. R. W. Longstaff, *Evidence of Conflation in Mark* (Society of Biblical Literature Dissertation Series 26; Missoula, Mont.: Scholars Press, 1977), believes that extra detail and vivid additions are a sign of secondariness and dependence.

23. The only way of getting around the problem of the minor agreements is by recourse to coincidental editing, oral tradition, and/or textual corruption. See W. D. Davies and D. C. Allison Jr., *The Gospel according to Saint Matthew* (International Critical Commentary; Edinburgh: Clark, 1988), 1:109–14.

24. See Orchard and Riley, *Order of the Synoptics*, part 1.

hypothesis, a case can be made on the basis of internal evidence for maintaining it as a possible solution to the synoptic problem. Nevertheless, internal literary criticism favors the Fourfold-Gospel Hypothesis in the great majority of cases.

Within the limits of this brief chapter it is not possible to do more than show that the internal evidence is unable to offer any agreed solution to the problem of the literary relationships between the Synoptic Gospels. It is therefore necessary to look beyond it to the other two criteria: the external evidence and the historical likelihood of the hypothesis adopted. There are grounds for thinking that the fundamental reason why these other criteria have been neglected by Markan priorists, and why the hopes of a solution have been pinned exclusively to internal evidence, is theological and not critical. The stubborn adherence to Markan priority in the face of all its weaknesses compels one to conclude that it has been regarded almost unconsciously as a dogma of scholarship over against the claims of the church to control the dogmatic interpretation of the Scriptures, for the critics seek always to offer an alternative explanation to that of church tradition and belief.[25]

---

25. Here we may call attention to W. R. Farmer's detailed analysis of the debate in the nineteenth and twentieth centuries: *The Synoptic Problem: A Critical Analysis* (New York: Macmillan, 1964). He notes that defenders of Markan priority were influenced by theological positions and "that 'extra-scientific' or 'nonscientific' factors exercised a deep influence in the development of a fundamentally misleading and false consensus" (190). While rejecting a conscious connection between Markan priority and evolutionary social theory, he nevertheless concludes "that the Marcan hypothesis exhibited features which commended itself to men who were disposed to place their trust in the capacity of science to foster the development of human progress" (179). Farmer is worth quoting, not merely because of his massive scholarship, but because on this subject he was forced slowly and painfully to change his mind.

If, then, the evidence favoring Markan priority were now to be seen as no longer compelling, there is reason to question whether the rejection of ancient Christian tradition about the origins of the Gospels may have been premature. And, in fact, during the past thirty years the hypothesis of Markan priority has been subjected to such a devastating scrutiny that it is no longer possible to use it as a sure basis for exegesis.[26] And if its basis is no longer certain, then it can no longer be used as an argument for the rejection of the historical evidence.

The Credibility of the Fourfold-Gospel Hypothesis

It is now time to give a positive answer to the question as to why Mark should have treated Matthew and Luke in the way the Markan priority hypothesis claims. The answer is this: Mark was never meant to be an independent Gospel. The reason for its existence is connected with the unfolding of the brilliant strategy of Paul and the sympathetic collaboration of Peter as they saw their mighty labors beginning to bear fruit. The tradition asserts explicitly that Mark is the result of a series of lectures given by Peter in Rome to a distinguished audience that included a number of high-ranking officers from the Roman Praetorium. The tradition is also explicit that Mark was on hand as Peter's aide; and because of the presence of the knights of Caesar's Praetorium,

---

26. As far back as 1976 J. A. T. Robinson noted, "The consensus frozen by the success of 'the fundamental solution' propounded by B. H. Streeter has begun to show signs of cracking. Though it is still the dominant hypothesis, encapsulated in the textbooks, its conclusions can no longer be taken for granted as among the 'assured results' of biblical criticism"; *Redating the New Testament* (Philadelphia: Westminster, 1976), 93. More recently, C. M. Tuckett, "Jesus and the Gospels," in *New Interpreter's Bible* (Nashville: Abingdon, 1995), 8:71–86, openly acknowledges that the standard arguments for the priority of Mark are "weak and inconclusive."

these lectures were suitable occasions for the use of shorthand writers of Greek to record his words. We are also told by Clement of Alexandria that the audience was so appreciative that they demanded to be given the text of what Peter had said, that Mark was able to satisfy them, and that, when Peter learned of their request, he took no action either to promote or to suppress the text of what he had said. This acquiescence strongly suggests that other Gospels must have been available in order to justify his taking no further interest in his own reminiscences of Jesus. As we have already suggested, Mark lacks the form of a book or a biography of a great man as understood at that time, for it is basically a series of personal anecdotes told in a graphic and colloquial style without literary grace and put together in zigzag fashion without introduction or conclusion.[27] The stories closely follow the wording and order first of one Gospel (Matthew) and then of the other (Luke), snaking from one to the other in a manner that betrays that the speaker must have had both of these Gospels before him when he spoke.

But what could have persuaded Peter (as the real author of Mark's Gospel) to act and speak in such a peculiar way? And why should his words have been recorded so meticulously? A reasonable explanation for such extraordinary action must be sought and is to be found in the critical condition of the churches of Peter and Paul in the final years of their apostolates. Their lives were drawing to a close, and there was still a great rift between the circumcision and noncircumcision parties. The Gospel of Matthew had already proved itself to be not only the manifesto of the church

---

27. Riley, *Order of the Synoptics,* 97, reminds us that "Mark wrote in a colloquial style, without great literary nicety. He was telling the stories again in the way that came naturally to him. The result was the lively manner of the speaker, rather than the thought-out arrangement of the professional writer."

of Jerusalem but also the fundamental document for the evangelization of the world. Paul, however, had found that it paid insufficient attention to the needs of his Gentile churches and urgently wanted to have a similar manifesto adapted to his own converts' requirements. He had found in Luke the ideal scholar and author for his purpose, and Luke had composed his Gospel during Paul's confinement in Caesarea, basically following the order and plan of Matthew but with a whole series of adaptations that made it the appropriate vehicle for the noncircumcision constituency of the church.

Since neither Luke nor Paul had been eyewitnesses of the life and ministry of Jesus, and since the tension between circumcision and noncircumcision was still at a precarious level, this Gospel of Luke might well have proved extremely divisive if published without the approval or at least the knowledge of Peter, the mediating leader of the Twelve and the most authoritative eyewitness of all. At the very outset of his apostolate, Paul had made a missionary pact with Peter, James, and John (Gal. 2), and what he now wanted was an acknowledgment from Peter that Luke's Gospel—that is, *Paul's* gospel (Rom. 2:16)—was fully consistent with the apostolic tradition found in Matthew. And since we learn from 1 Peter (5:12-13) that both Peter and his disciple Mark were in Rome when Paul was a prisoner there in 62, and since we find that the disciples Luke and Mark are mentioned together in Colossians and Philemon (which were, according to tradition, also written from Rome about the same time), it is reasonable to conclude that the purpose of Peter's lectures as we find them in the Gospel of Mark was to give Paul and his churches (and Peter's churches too) the assurance that the Gospel of Luke could validly stand comparison with the Gospel of Matthew. The Gospel of Mark is Peter's declaration that Luke is faithful to the apostolic tradition, and Mark itself is therefore to be seen as the document that draws together the respective traditions of the churches of the circumcision and the noncircumcision, thus sealing the unity of the western churches of Peter and Paul.

This mediating and unifying action of Peter in linking the Gospels of Matthew and Luke together, using his personal reminiscences of the Lord's words and deeds, also explains and justifies the tradition that puts the Gospel of Mark between those of Matthew and Luke. For although Griesbach was right in asserting that Luke was composed before Mark, it was the harmonizing and binding quality of Mark's Gospel that provided the approbation necessary for Luke to find general acceptance in all the churches. It also explains why the Gospel of Mark practically disappeared from view for several centuries thereafter, for simply by being the link between Matthew and Luke it had fulfilled the original purpose of both Peter and Paul.

Conclusion

History teaches us that the Gospels evolved in the church to meet the need for information about Jesus in the Christian assembly, which wanted to know what Jesus said and did. As P. Carrington observes:[28]

> It is not realistic thinking . . . [to hold] the curious assumption that personal contact with the first generation disciples mysteriously ceased at some primary stage before the Gospel material took standardised oral and written form; or, alternatively, that any reliable memory of the life and teaching of Jesus has been erased from their minds. . . . Oral tradition was not unorganised conversation or casual reminiscence, provided by unnamed and unknown preach-

---

28. P. Carrington, *According to Mark* (Cambridge: Cambridge University Press, 1960), 12.

ers working without any control; or else the work of local teachers in undocumented non-apostolic churches manipulating material the origin of which was obscure.

The earliest Christian materials were thus created in the Jewish Christian community with its continuous history from pre-Christian times and with its living tradition, a tradition that at all times was embodied in persons, not in anonymous communities.

Here, then, we have a satisfactory reason for the creation of the Gospel of Mark. It was never intended to be a rival to the Gospels of Matthew and Luke. It had only a limited purpose, but because Mark was known to reflect the personal reminiscences of Peter, the Christian church took care to also preserve his memories and they were elevated to the third Gospel by accident so to speak and despite the modesty of Peter himself.

In this hypothesis we have the only scientific answer to the question, "Why Mark?" Unlike the fantastic hypotheses thought up by exponents of Markan priority, which cannot be directly refuted because they are all located in the blank tunnel period, the Fourfold-Gospel Hypothesis respects and accepts the real life situation of the universal church in the years 30–67 and agrees with the known history of the apostolic churches at all key points.

To conclude, the Fourfold-Gospel Hypothesis fulfills the three essential criteria for a definitive solution to the synoptic problem: It is the only solution that conforms to the historical and patristic evidence; it meets the internal data at least as well as the Markan priority hypothesis, and often much better; and it is the only solution that explains the need for three Synoptic Gospels—no fewer and no more.

3

The Making
of the Gospels

THE GOSPELS WERE ALL composed in the lifetimes of the apostles.
This being the case, we are now in a position to make legitimate
speculations about the thoughts and motives of the principal historical characters of this period in light of the existing canonical
writings. In the period between 180 and 220, Matthew and John
(who were apostles) and Mark and Luke (who were disciples of
apostles) were everywhere regarded as the authors of the four
books that, even as early as 150, were commonly called Gospels
(cf. Justin, *Apology* 1.66: "which are called gospels," *ha kaleitai
euangelia*). It was this tradition of the church regarding the apostolic composition of the Gospels that found embodiment in the
Greek manuscripts and soon afterward in the Latin translations,
even in the titles (i.e., superscriptions) of the separate Gospels,
the original form of which in all probability was *kata Matthaion,
kata Loukan,* etc.[1] The oldest patristic witnesses all agree that

---

1. Codex Vaticanus (ca. 350) has as titles of the four Gospels *kata
   Matthaion*, etc. That the Latin equivalent, *secundum Matthaeum*, origi-
   nated with the Greek is shown by presence of the Greek form *cata
   Matthaeum* in the manuscripts of the Old Latin version.

Matthew, Mark, Luke, and John wrote the books bearing their respective names and that the ultimate source of Mark's Gospel was Peter's oral preaching. The rise of this tradition from actual facts adequate to explain its origin is all the more necessary because there is nothing in the books themselves that would necessarily have given rise to the unanimous tradition regarding their authorship. It follows, then, that the tradition associated with the four Gospels from the time when they began to circulate is based, not upon learned conjectures but upon facts that at the time were incontrovertible.

The Composition of Matthew

The Gospel of Matthew was probably composed in Greek, because this was the only appropriate language for use by a church that saw the whole world as the field of its evangelization. Internal evidence shows that Matthew was the right document to meet the needs of the Jerusalem church as described in the first twelve chapters of the Acts of the Apostles. Its first concern was to prove from the canonical books of the Jews that Jesus was the Christ and that he came not to destroy but to fulfill the law of Moses (Matt. 5:17). This book also deals with liturgical, ritual, moral, and social questions in a manner that met the anxieties and needs of a Christian minority in the midst of a hostile Jewish environment. It was written for a church that made universalist claims (Matt. 8:11–12; 28:16–20) but had not yet begun in earnest its mission to the Gentiles. It was this Gospel alone that was available to Paul during his three missionary journeys to convert the Greeks.

For a literate people like the Jews, recording the life and teachings of Jesus in a book was no novelty. Thus it is highly probable that the Jerusalem church made one of its highest priorities to formulate the teaching of the master not only in oral form but also in writing. It is vitally important to remember that it was always the Twelve, in close association with Peter, who strictly controlled the teaching of the Jerusalem church, that is, the teaching coming directly from Jesus himself. Because of their unique relationship to Jesus during his earthly ministry, they alone possessed the full story of what Jesus said and did. It is therefore sensible to infer that the apostles would have felt compelled to put down and into circulation their memories of Jesus while these were still fresh and fully relevant to their immediate situation.

Based on the research chronicled above, it is reasonable to conclude that the Gospel of Matthew is no more and no less than the written record that the apostles had personally received from Jesus during the years they accompanied him in his ministry. In order to pass on accurately this oral tradition they had to make a synthesis of his sayings and deeds that would comprise all that was immediately important for the situation of the primitive church in Jerusalem and Judea. The Gospel of Matthew is the proof that this task was faithfully carried out. For our present purpose the most interesting facts regarding the composition of Matthew are the following:[2]

1. Matthew is primarily concerned with matters in which the first Christians were deeply and passionately interested, for example, the genealogy of Jesus, his relation to the Torah and to its rabbinic interpretation, and his fulfillment of the Old Testament prophecies about the Messiah.
2. It assumes that its readers were familiar with the customs and views of the scribes, Pharisees, and Sadducees. It never explains who they are.
3. It further assumes that its readers know why these groups were so hostile to Jesus and that they were aware of the

---

2. Cf. B. Orchard and H. Riley, *The Order of the Synoptics* (Macon, Ga.: Mercer University Press, 1987), 233–35.

conflict between the Pharisees' interpretation of the law of Moses and Jesus' teaching.

4. It reflects a certain tension concerning the payment of the temple tax.
5. It indicates a situation in which its readers were used to being harassed by the Jerusalem officials.
6. It lacks any evidence that the church had already started officially to evangelize the Gentiles, though of course it contains many foreshadowings of what was to come.
7. It indicates that the social milieu of Jesus' time was still intact when Matthew was written (see the phrase "even unto this day" in Matt. 27:8; 28:15).
8. It contained various themes that appealed to the religious patriotism of Jews but had no appeal to Gentiles, such as Jesus' succeeding Moses as the giver of the new law.
9. The text poses no obstacle to the tradition that the author was the apostle Matthew, the former tax collector, who would probably have been the best qualified by education and worldly experience to collect and edit the sayings of Jesus into a coherent whole in the Greek language.
10. The internal evidence is not opposed to a date before 70, even before Paul's first missionary journey (47–49), that is, prior to the departure of Peter from Jerusalem about 44 (cf. Acts 12).

In terms of the essential content of the Gospel, Matthew begins abruptly with the assertion that Jesus is the Christ and proves by his genealogy that he is the son of David by legal adoption on the part of Joseph, whose fiancée Mary had unexpectedly conceived by the power of the Holy Spirit (1:1–25). Matthew stresses the importance of the witness of John the Baptist, Jesus' prophesied forerunner, whom the whole nation revered as a prophet of God (3:1–17; 11:2–19). Jesus' claim to have authority both to fulfill and to complete the law of Moses made it essential to show that he was superior to Moses and greater than Jonah and Solomon (5:17–48; 12:38–42). The construction of five great discourses (5:1–7:29; 10:1–42; 13:1–58; 18:1–35; 24:1–25:46) show Jesus remolding the law given to Moses. These discourses are interspersed by a carefully chosen selection of story units illustrating various aspects of the person and work of Christ. Matthew's Gospel also makes it clear that the priestly leaders of the Jewish people were responsible for the crucifixion of Jesus, who was condemned to death for his claim to be the Son of God and his further claim that his enemies would one day see him coming on the clouds of heaven, in fulfillment of the prophecy of Daniel (26:64).

Thus we see how Matthew can be viewed as the Gospel of the church of Jerusalem and the true prototype of the Gospel genre. We also see how the first document of the Christian church about Jesus the Messiah could have evolved within the Jerusalem church itself in response to its existential needs. The formation of Matthew's Gospel probably took place in the first decade of the church's life, that is, before 44, and thus not only before 1–2 Thessalonians and Galatians but probably before Paul's second visit to Jerusalem "after fourteen years" (Gal. 2:1; cf. Acts 11:27–30; 12:25).

Luke's Use of Matthew

Precisely because of its orientation toward the Christian Jews of Palestine, the Gospel of Matthew came to be seen by Paul and his disciple Luke as a not wholly suitable instrument for the evangelization of the Gentiles, although by virtue of its being the Gospel of the original church of Jerusalem and of its having the authority of the twelve apostles it was irrevocably the fundamental document of the Christian faith. Toward the end of his third missionary journey, Paul therefore invited his disciple Luke to give some thought to composing a new version of the Gospel message that would cater to the intellectual and spiritual requirements of his new churches. The most appropriate time for Paul to have set Luke to work would have been during Paul's imprisonment at Caesarea in 58–60, as described in Acts 21–26, where the "we" passages indicate the presence of Luke. It will now be instructive to investigate the sort of guidelines that Paul would have laid down for Luke to observe in the construction of his new Gospel.[3]

In the first place, given the authority wielded by the Twelve over the tradition, such a project would have been inconceivable without the personal initiative and the positive approbation and support of an apostle with the authority of Paul, who had been designated by Jesus himself as the apostle to the Gentiles (Acts 9:15). According to the Fourfold-Gospel Hypothesis, the Gospel of Matthew was the Gospel of the primitive church of Jerusalem, that is, the church of the twelve apostles and the authentic document of the tradition received from Christ himself. Written by the apostle Matthew, with the aid no doubt of the rest of the Twelve including Peter, it recorded the person and teaching of Jesus in magisterial and monumental form. It was unthinkable that it should ever be outmoded or superseded, and by the year 58 it may well have been in circulation for as much as fifteen years. Thus it would have enjoyed an inalienable and unassailable position not only in the Jewish Christian churches but also among all the churches established from Jerusalem, including those founded

---

3. The following material has been adapted from B. Orchard, "Some Reflections on the Relationship of Luke to Matthew," in *Jesus, the Gospels, and the Church: Essays in Honor of William R. Farmer*, ed. E. P. Sanders (Macon, Ga.: Mercer University Press, 1987), 33–46.

by Paul himself, since he praises highly their imitation of the churches of God in Judea (1 Thess. 2:14).

Since there is clear evidence not only of Paul's use of the Matthean tradition but also of his possession of the actual Greek text of Matthew, it follows that both its strengths and its weaknesses as an instrument for the evangelization of the Gentiles were well known to him; and we too, as a result of hindsight, are able to understand his desire to have a new presentation of the identical message, one that would satisfy the needs and aspirations of the mass of Greek converts who had been educated outside the Mosaic law and in an entirely different culture. Paul saw that they needed a positive presentation of Christianity in terms that would be both congenial and credible to them as Greeks. The Gospel of Matthew represented the indigenous Christianity of Judea; but what Paul was looking for was a new perspective, a manifesto that would not only respect the essential message of Matthew but would at the same time remove its preoccupation with matters of little interest or relevance to Greeks, such as Christ's attitude to the Mosaic law or rabbinic subtleties, and would instead lay stress on his universal salvific mission. Yet given the invariable conservatism of Christians in favor of the tradition, no ordinary Christian would dare claim that the Gospel of Matthew could either be improved or that anyone might add anything to it. But if, as we believe, Paul was actually going to commission Luke to rework the whole Gospel message for the benefit of his own Greek churches, he would have to guard against the upsurge of a storm of criticism from the circumcision party that would be difficult to overcome and that might even endanger the peace and unity of the whole church. Nevertheless, he must have felt justified in taking the risk, since he had received a mandate from the Lord himself to preach the Gospel to the Greeks.

Among those whom Luke likely interviewed for his new Gospel

would have been all the important figures in the church of Jerusalem at that time, including James of Jerusalem (martyred in 62), the younger relatives of Jesus, a number of the women who had ministered to him (Luke 8:2–3), and of course scores of persons up and down Judea and Galilee who had seen and heard and spoken to and with Jesus (Luke 1:1–4). Since, however, neither Luke nor Paul personally knew Jesus during his lifetime, neither could bear firsthand witness to the truth of any of the stories told about him or even of the extra details Luke was able to add to the stories in Matthew after his research. Thus the Gospel of Luke would never possess the authority wielded by the Gospel of Matthew unless Luke or Paul could find one of the Twelve to authenticate it. And so far as we know the only apostles still active in the Mediterranean world at that time were John and Peter, around whose figure Luke was also weaving his account of the first fifteen years of the church's life (Acts 1–12). If Luke could persuade Peter to confirm the truth and validity of his presentation, his Gospel could then circulate with the same authority as Matthew's. But before we record the success of his quest for approbation, we must look into Luke's method of gathering together all the materials he had acquired by personal research during Paul's incarceration at Caesarea in 58–60 and then writing his Gospel.

According to the Fourfold-Gospel Hypothesis, Luke had Matthew before him as his exemplar. Now the Gospel of Matthew is, in fact, a beautiful literary whole, and from its opening genealogy of Christ to the final instruction of Christ its theme is the messiahship of Jesus and the proclamation of his death and resurrection to the whole world. Its style and content are, of course, definitely Hebraic, as noted by Papias at the beginning of the second century: "Matthew composed the sayings in a Hebrew style." Luke, however, is a literary masterpiece of another kind. It is composed in the kind of writing that a cultured citizen of the Greco-Roman world would expect to find in the biography of a great statesman or national hero. That is, of the four canonical Gospels, Luke conforms most clearly to the contemporary convention of *bios* literature—the genre of ancient biographies. The biographer was expected to extol the virtues of his hero by relating how his subject had been favored at birth by the gods; how he had compelled the admiration of everyone by his moral and physical excellence; how he had won the unsolicited acclaim of his fellow citizens by his exploits on behalf of his nation; how he had courageously confronted his enemies' jealousy and enmity; and how in his noble death he had displayed all the qualities of his life at their best. Finally, there had to be an epilogue recounting the lasting benefits of his virtuous life, thus proving that he had not lived in vain and had left behind a glorious name.

Broadly speaking, Luke respected the main structure of Matthew and conformed to it; that is, both use the same order for the birth narrative, the mission of John the Baptist, the Galilean ministry, Jesus' ministry in Jerusalem, his passion and death, and the resurrection appearances. The main divergences of order are not numerous but are significant and can best be followed in Bernard Orchard's Greek synopsis.[4] The first problem in applying Luke to Matthew arises at Matthew 4:23, which leads up to the Sermon on the Mount; and here one must decide whether to parallel Matthew's Sermon on the Mount with Luke's Sermon on the Plain. Since, however, both sermons have a similar beginning, middle, and ending, the decision to consider Matthew 4:24–7:27 parallel to Luke 6:12–49 has far-reaching effects on all further parallels down to Matthew 14:1. Among the consequences to be noted is that Luke has brought forward the parables discourse

---

4. B. Orchard, *A Synopsis of the Four Gospels in Greek* (Macon, Ga.: Mercer University Press/Edinburgh: Clark, 1983).

(8:4–18) so that it is no longer parallel to Matthew's. This decision, in turn, makes it possible for Luke to parallel his rudimentary missionary discourse (9:2–5) with Matthew's (10:5–15) and later on to parallel the other major Matthean discourses.

At this point Luke observed that Matthew divided the Galilean ministry into three phases between the choosing of the Twelve (8:2) and Jesus' departure (19:1–2): (a) 8:2–11:1; (b) 11:2–14:12 (which happens to be the interval when the disciples were out preaching on their own); and (c) 14:13–19:2. Luke, however, made this division his own in a rather different fashion by abbreviating all three divisions in varying degrees: (a) 7:1–9:6; (b) 9:7–10a; and (c) 9:10b–51. The most striking difference is that Luke reduced the interval of the apostles' absence from Matthew's three chapters to just three verses (9:7–9), in which he described Herod's bewilderment at all the "goings on" in his kingdom. How did Luke achieve this rearrangement while remaining faithful to the general framework of Matthew? Chiefly by means of the creation of his central section, which he situated at 9:51 (= Matt. 19:1), when according to Matthew Jesus left Galilee for good and ultimately for Jerusalem. Even for Matthew this journey was somewhat indeterminate and leisurely between Matthew 19:3 and the arrival of Jesus at Jericho (20:29–34). Luke, however, decided to make this section (9:51–18:14) an important feature of his Gospel, for it occupies about one-third of its total length. For him too it is a journey section—a long and indeterminate journey, it is true, but one into which he pours almost everything that he withdrew from other portions of Matthew's Gospel: the Sermon on the Mount, the parables discourse, the missionary discourse, the material that Matthew used to fill the space while the apostles were away evangelizing (Matt. 11:1–13:58 + 14:1–12), and Matthew's discourses (8:1–34; 23:1–39; 24:1–25:46).

Thus Luke's central section became the storehouse for all those sayings of Jesus that Luke took out of their Matthean context, save for a few minor exceptions (e.g., the Lukan doublets of 8:16–18 or Matt. 10:17–22 = Luke 21:12–19). It is clear that while Luke intended to preserve the main chronological framework of Matthew, he did not intend that in his Gospel the action of Jesus should be held up by the five long discourses that we find in Matthew. The creation of such a section was for Luke really the only way in which he could remain faithful to the tradition established by Matthew and yet be able to introduce into his Gospel the new perspectives that Paul required. On the other hand, the central section gave him a number of new options, for editorially he was now free to move stories and sayings around to suit the new pattern; he could now introduce new anecdotes into the central section (e.g., 9:52–56), or he could insert them into his newly streamlined narrative (e.g., the miraculous catch in 5:1–11 or the widow's mite in 21:1–4). The central section also allowed him to retain and yet give less prominence to some of Jesus' strictures on his fellow Jews (e.g., their exclusion from the kingdom in Luke 13:28–29 = Matt. 8:11–12 or Jesus' condemnation of the scribes and Pharisees in Luke 11:37–54 = Matt. 23:1–36).

By streamlining his account of the Galilean ministry, by skillfully manipulating the pericope order, by making full use of the central section to retain almost every saying of Jesus, and by skillfully introducing new material here and there, Luke was able to change the whole emphasis of the Gospel into a demonstration of the good fortune of the Gentiles in being given equality by Jesus with the original chosen people, but without humiliating the Jews still further. Thus Luke was splendidly right in his Acts of the Apostles when he illustrated the history of the development of the apostolic church in terms of the leadership of the two greatest of its figures, Peter and Paul. If this thesis is correct, then the Gospel of Matthew is to be viewed as the manifesto of the primitive church of Jerusalem, presided over and guided by Peter in the critical years of its formation. Matthew is thus the blueprint or handbook for all future expansion, and the church it was written for was the model for all the churches of the world that issued from it, including those established by Paul. We have very little certain knowledge about the foundations of the other apostles; but thanks to Luke we have a great deal of information about the churches Paul founded and about the Gospel he preached, and in their writings we have a priceless contemporary account of how they set about the evangelization of the Roman Empire. Luke's Gospel was constructed to be Paul's special teaching instrument, and in the Acts (and in the letters of Paul) we have the background necessary to understand the connection between Luke and Matthew. Under the guidance of Paul and in light of his experience among the Greeks, Luke was able to restate the main teaching of Matthew in a form and style that appealed to the Greek mind and heart.

The Markan Synthesis

The complementarity of Luke to Matthew is the mirror of the complementarity of the mission of Paul to that of Peter, as seen in the Book of Acts. And the document that binds together these two distinct yet complementary Gospels is the Gospel of Mark, who according to the most ancient tradition was the *hermēneutēs* of Peter. J. J. Griesbach, to his great honor, saw this in a brilliant insight, but at the literary level only; he failed to understand what lay behind and underneath the bare literary relationship, namely the union of heart and mind of the two founders of western Christianity and the completion of their grand strategy for the church. The unifying role of the Gospel of Mark was thus a necessary concomitant of Luke's use of Matthew. Because of its secondary character, Luke needed the approval of an eyewitness apostle to gain proper accreditation in the church. Clement of Alexandria has recorded the very ancient tradition that the Gospel of Mark is neither more nor less than the discourses of Peter given in Rome and recorded by his disciple Mark. And if we combine this piece of information with Griesbach's insight that Mark had the Gospels of Matthew and Luke in his hands when composing his own Gospel, we have found what looks like the final piece that completes the "jigsaw" of the synoptic problem. That is, Peter himself was the apostolic eyewitness who provided the accreditation for the Gospel of Luke by personally comparing it with the Gospel of Matthew as he gave his own oral version of the stories common to both, at which he himself had been present in person.

In the most ancient text to discuss expressly the order of the composition of the four Gospels (*Ecclesiastical History* 6.14), Clement of Alexandria is quoted as saying that the Gospel of Mark came after the two Gospels with genealogies and that it resulted from public lectures given by Peter himself to a Roman audience, which, as Clement informs us elsewhere (*Adumbrationes in epistolas canonicas* on 1 Peter 5:13), contained a number of Caesar's "knights." Clement also added (*Ecclesiastical History* 6.14) that the large audience begged Mark to write down what Peter had said, and that Mark, after some persuasion, yielded to their request. Clement concluded his account by relating that when Peter found out about this, he made no effort either to forbid or to promote its circulation. Thus Clement, and other ancient witnesses, understood Mark's function to have been simply that of reporting Peter's words with total accuracy. That is, Mark was not the author of the Gospel but simply the agent of its publication, because all of this material came from Peter's own memories of what Jesus had said and done and because what Mark did was to retrieve faithfully, as Peter's amanuensis, what the latter had spoken on certain special occasions. These are the basic historical facts around which all of the internal evidence will be found to fit exactly.

What, then, would the preparation of Peter's lectures have involved?[5] We must assume that the lectures were given in the atrium of some large private house, quite possibly during the weekly Christian assembly. It would seem that the Gospel book that Luke brought with him to Rome must have been in the normal format of that era, namely, the scroll. Matthew, slightly shorter than Luke, must also originally have been in a scroll format.[6] Peter's plan was to take the scroll of Luke and compare it with the scroll of Matthew in light of his own eyewitness recollections of the ministry of Jesus, beginning with John the Baptist, whose disciple he had been, and ending with the discovery of the empty tomb. Our Gospel of Mark is therefore the result of the combined effort of Peter and his disciple Mark, who was at Peter's side as he delivered his lectures and was the person responsible for seeing that a true record was kept of what Peter said.

We can also infer that Peter switched between the two scrolls by Matthew and Luke and that he naturally tended to follow the order of whichever scroll he had in his hand. Thus, despite the different order of pericopes in Matthew and Luke, Peter never goes back to some passage that he has previously passed over in either scroll, but always goes steadily forward alternately through each. That is why, for instance, Mark does not retell the centurion's slave pericope (Matt. 8:5–13), for Peter has moved on to Luke 6:20, which corresponds to Matthew 12:15, though the scroll of Matthew was still open at 4:25. Peter must have noted that Matthew 12:15–21 was curiously reminiscent of Matthew 4:25; so instead

---

5. The following discussion is indebted to Orchard and Riley, *Order of the Synoptics*, 269–74.

6. B. M. Metzger, *The Text of the New Testament* (Oxford: Oxford University Press, 1968), 5–6, reminds us that "the Gospel of Luke and the Book of Acts—the two longest books in the New Testament—would each have filled an ordinary papyrus roll of 31 or 32 feet in length."

of continuing with Luke 6:20, he passes over all of Luke 6:20–8:3 and continues with Matthew 12:22 until he reaches Matthew 13:1 (= Luke 8:4).

We must remember that Peter knew the Gospel of Matthew practically by heart, and on his first reading of Luke's scroll he must have recognized the extent of its dependence on the Gospel of Matthew and therefore framed his lectures accordingly. Thus the analysis of Mark in relation to Luke-with-Matthew will show us the steps the speaker took to organize his material, for he did not accomplish his task in one lecture but took no less than five, each of which would have lasted from twenty-five to forty minutes (Mark 1:2–3:19; 3:20–6:13; 6:14–10:1; 10:2–13:37; 14:1–16:8).

From the start, the speaker determined to confine himself to those pericopes where Matthew and Luke have for the most part common material and are generally in parallel, that is, between Matthew 3:1 (= Luke 3:1) and Matthew 28:10 (= Luke 24:12). Thus Peter omitted the birth and resurrection narratives, the whole of Luke's central section, and both great sermons; but he also adopted Luke's summary version of (a) Matthew's missionary discourse (Luke 9:3–5 = Mark 6:8–11), (b) Matthew's discourse on community (Luke 9:46–48 = Mark 9:33–37), (c) Matthew's parables discourse, with some Markan additions (Luke 8:4–18 = Mark 4:1–25), and (d) Matthew's main eschatological discourse (Luke 21:5–36 = Mark 13:1–37). On the whole, Peter included only personal memories in the form of short stories at the telling of which he was present; but he also omitted Lukan glosses and Lukan reconstructions. He decided, however, to include not only events that Luke had taken from Matthew, but also certain events that he thought Luke should not have omitted from Matthew (e.g., Matt. 14:22–15:39); he also added two or three minor stories of his own that are not recorded by the others (e.g., Mark 7:31–37). He also sometimes restored Matthean stories that Luke regarded as duplicates, when the latter inserts a similar story in his central section (e.g., the fig tree parable in Mark 11:20–26 = Matt. 21:19–22 = Luke 13:6–9). Peter also felt free to add little asides from time to time (e.g., Mark 7:19). It would therefore be necessary for him to have gone through both scrolls in advance and mark carefully what he was going to include, what he was going to omit, and also the exact point where he was going to switch from one scroll to the other. This was a straightforward editorial process.

During Peter's talks, he would have been assisted by some secretaries and other members of his entourage. And since a scroll needs to be held in both hands at once, the right hand unrolling, the left hand rolling, the speaker would need to have at least one secretary close at hand to pass him the scroll in the first place and then to take it back and hand him the other whenever he decided to switch. The audience would of course have observed Mark handing the scrolls to Peter and receiving them back from him and so naturally would have asked him later for a written copy. Meanwhile, assuming that shorthand writers were present, probably two in number, they would have been seated near at hand taking down the lecture.

The theme of the first lecture was the proclamation of Jesus' message in Galilee. Peter began at Luke 3:1 (= Matt. 3:1) and then followed carefully to Luke 6:19, omitting Luke 3:7–9 (= Matt. 3:7–10); 3:10–14; 3:19–20 (a Lukan editorial addition to Matthew); 3:23–38; and 4:16–30 (the Nazareth visit); and adding Mark 1:16–20 (parallel to Matt. 4:18–22, which Luke omitted in favor of his 5:1–11, which Mark omits). The speaker then followed the order of Luke faithfully down to Luke 6:19, paralleling Matthew 4:23–25, though he preferred Matthew's order of units in the latter verses, namely, at Mark 3:7–19. The speaker felt free to harmonize Luke with Matthew, to omit Lukan glosses, and to prefer Matthew's wording to Luke's at certain points. He reveals himself to be fully conversant with both Gospels. He has now arrived at Luke 6:20 (= Mark 3:19). At this decisive moment in the Galilean ministry, he decided to pause, ending with Mark 3:19, thus sounding the keynote for the second lecture. This was a convenient place to stop, since Luke had already gone ahead with his incorporation of Matthean material down to Matthew 12:15–21, a passage reminiscent of Matthew 4:25, at which point the scroll of Matthew was still open.

For the second lecture—the development of the opposition to Jesus—the scrolls have been turned forward, bypassing both of the great sermons and all of Luke 6:20–8:3. Peter now turns to Matthew, taking into account that Luke had already reached Matthew 12:15–21, and opens with 3:20–30 (= Matt. 12:22–30) and continued with 3:31–35 (= Matt. 12:46–50), thus following Matthew until he reached the parables at Matthew 13:1, which enabled him to return to Luke 8:4–18 = Mark 4:1–25. At this point Peter added his own unique parable of the seed growing secretly (Mark 4:26–29) and then went back to the order of Matthew for the mustard seed and Jesus' use of parables (Mark 4:30–34 = Matt. 13:31–33). From this point onward, the speaker followed Luke down to Luke 9:6 (= Mark 6:12–13). Again, he continued to go forward in each scroll, and never backward, despite the variations in the order of Matthew and Luke. The lecture ended at a natural break, when the scrolls of Matthew and Luke are about to become parallel again (after Mark 6:13).

The theme of the third lecture is that of preparing the Twelve for the passion of Jesus; it opens with the story of Herod's sinister interest in Jesus (Luke 9:7–9 = Matt. 14:1–2 = Mark 6:14–16), which fills in the gap between the sending out of the Twelve (Luke 9:6) and their return (Luke 9:10), though Luke omitted Matthew's account of the martyrdom of the Baptist. Peter, however, thought this ought to have figured in Luke's account (seeing that it is in

Matthew), and he decided to restore it at Mark 6:17–29, at the same time considerably amplifying the details of Matthew 14:3–12. The speaker retold the feeding of the five thousand (Mark 6:32–44), following Luke and Matthew, but when he came to Luke's great omission he decided to restore it fully to his own narrative, Mark 6:45–8:21 (= Matt. 14:22–16:12). (Luke had, in fact, tucked a few verses of this material, namely Matthew 16:1–4, 5–12, into his central section at Luke 12:54–56 and 12:1.) Peter, however, could not at this point resist an impulse to introduce a healing story of his own, namely, Mark 8:22–26. He then followed Luke and Matthew together down to the discourse on community, Matthew 18:1–5 (= Luke 9:46–48 = Mark 9:33–37), except that where Luke omitted Jesus' rebuke of Peter, he restored it—though he did not restore Matthew's temple tax anecdote (17:24–27) that Luke omitted, because it did not concern his Roman audience. At this point Mark inserts a saying of Jesus about salt (Mark 9:50b), which made a suitable conclusion to his summary of Matthew's discourse on community and concludes this section with his departure from Galilee (Luke 9:51 = Matt. 19:1–2 = Mark 10:1).

The fourth lecture details the various confrontations of Jesus with his enemies on the way to Jerusalem and in the Holy City itself. So Peter (Mark), having decided to omit the whole of Luke's central section, began by restoring Matthew's teaching about divorce pericope (19:3–12), perhaps omitted by Luke because it was an example of rabbinic exegesis unfamiliar to Greeks (cf. Luke 16:18). But when Luke rejoined Matthew at Luke 18:15, Peter went steadily through Luke's scroll. As Matthew lacks it, so Peter too omits Luke 19:1–10 (Jesus and Zachaeus) and 19:11–27 (parable of the minas). He also omitted Jesus' weeping over Jerusalem (Luke 19:41–44) and rearranged the order of Matthew 21:12–22 = Mark 11:12–26. He omitted Matthew's parable of the marriage feast (22:1–14), perhaps because Luke has a similar story in his central section (Luke 14:15–24). He also restored Matthew 22:34–40 with his own special version of the lawyer's question (12:28–34, which Luke transferred to his central section in order to provide an introduction to his good Samaritan parable. Further on, at Luke 20:45–47, Peter took over the substance of Luke's abbreviated and truncated version of Matthew 23:1–36 (condemnation of the scribes and Pharisees) at Mark 12:38–40, with the difference that he omitted all the sayings that Luke had transferred to his central section (11:38–52). Peter also decided to retain the Lukan widow's mite unit as being of interest to his Gentile audience (Mark 12:41–44 = Luke 21:1–4). Peter now moved on to the eschatological discourse (Mark 13:1–37 = Luke 21:5–33 = Matt. 24:1–25:46) and followed Luke through this discourse, but brought back Matthew 24:23–28, which Luke had transferred to his central section at Luke 17:23–24. Ignoring the rest of Matthew's discourse, he complemented Luke's partial summary of Matthew with Mark 13:32–37. Though Luke adds two verses of explanation of Jesus' movements, our speaker ended his lecture with the above short summary.

The fifth lecture was exclusively devoted to the passion narrative and closely followed both Luke and Matthew. The Markan narrator (Peter) restored the anointing in Bethany (Matt. 26:6–13 = Mark 14:3–9), omitted by Luke, whose anointing story is at Luke 7:36–50. He preferred Matthew's arrangement of several pericopes where Luke changed his order, but the detail need not detain us here. The significant thing is that Peter ended his account at Mark 16:8 at the exact point where Matthew and Luke are about to commence their respective and entirely different accounts of the resurrection appearances of Jesus. This sudden ending, when related to Matthew and Luke, cannot be fortuitous, but is surely calculated even in its abruptness. The speaker stopped where his own personal eyewitness of the events of Jesus' earthly life ended, which was also the point at which the other two evangelists decided to introduce their independent resurrection stories. Peter's witness to the life of Jesus in his mortal flesh was now complete. This was all that Paul needed; he did not need to ask for Peter's witness to the risen Christ (cf. 1 Cor. 15:5), as the Lord had also blessed him with similar and perhaps even greater visions. Peter had now completed in a concise, restrained, and workmanlike manner the task that Paul and Luke had invited him to undertake, by witnessing to the substantial harmony and accuracy of Luke with Matthew over the total period of his own personal earthly contact with Jesus.

Since Mark was able to retrieve the actual text without difficulty, this would argue that shorthand writers must have been present to record the lectures. This need not surprise us since the shorthand recording of public statements of senators and prominent officials was commonplace in first-century Rome; indeed, it had been a recognized practice ever since the time of Cicero a hundred years earlier. At any rate, Clement of Alexandria makes it clear that Mark was able to come by a verbatim report of what Peter had said, since Mark was able to supply the text on request. Furthermore, the Gospel of Mark is in no way the smooth product of a skilled author seated at his desk, but has all the vividness and peculiar turns of speech that one finds in actual transcripts of live speeches. It was surely such peculiarities of direct and unedited speech that aroused the early criticisms of Mark's Gospel that the Elder of Papias was at pains to excuse.

With Paul still living in his own hired lodgings under house arrest, probably with a Praetorian soldier to guard him while awaiting the result of his appeal to Caesar, and with Peter taking all this trouble to support the Gospel written by Luke for the furtherance of the mission to which Paul had been called, there need be no surprise that Peter's lectures aroused great enthusiasm and prompted some of his audience to demand copies of them without delay. Paul and his assistants could now boast that "the salvation given to the Gentiles" (Acts 28:28) had its own special document to proclaim it—a document partly independent of, partly parallel to, and partly dependent upon the Gospel of Matthew, the Gospel of the original church of Jerusalem. And Mark's edition of Peter's words was now the tangible record of that achievement. No wonder that church tradition inserted the Gospel of Mark between the Gospels of Matthew and Luke as a reminder that it was the work of Mark recording the oral recommendation of Peter that had made possible the acceptance of Luke's Gospel on equal terms with Matthew's in the Christian world without danger of further controversy (cf. 2 Peter 1:1).

As for the subsequent history of Mark's Gospel, Peter took no particular interest in its recovery, for it was perhaps for him little more than a device of his secretary Mark, in response to popular request, to satisfy his hearers. As long as Peter was alive, it seems to have circulated privately; but after his martyrdom, Mark himself probably published it as an act of *pietas* to the memory of his old master. In doing so, he probably added the last twelve verses to make a more fitting and rounded conclusion to Peter's witness to the life and death of Jesus. According to an old tradition, Mark took his Gospel with him when he went to Alexandria; and at least until the end of the second century it remained very much in the shadow of the Gospel of Matthew. But Augustine of Hippo viewed it as the document that unified the Matthean conception of Jesus the Messiah King with the Lukan and Pauline view of Jesus as the High Priest and Savior of the world, though the peculiar circumstances of its origin appear to have been entirely forgotten in the intervening centuries.

The Background of John

The Gospel of John occupies the last place among the four canonical Gospels. Although in many ancient manuscripts this

Gospel was, on account of the apostolic dignity of its author, inserted immediately after or even before the Gospel of Matthew, the position it occupies today was from the beginning the most usual and the most approved. As to its contents, the Gospel of John is a narrative of the life of Jesus from his baptism to his resurrection and his self-manifestation in the midst of his disciples. The chronicle falls naturally into four sections: the prologue (1:1–18) contains a brief epitome of the whole Gospel in the doctrine of the incarnation of the Eternal Word; the first part (1:19–12:50) recounts the public life of Jesus from his baptism to the eve of his passion; the second part (13:1–21:23) relates the history of the passion and resurrection of the Savior; and a short epilogue (21:23–25) refers to the great mass of the Savior's words and works that are not recorded in the Gospel. The author follows the historical order of events, but he also displays a special concern to determine the exact timing and connection of the various events in this chronological framework. This is apparent at the very beginning of his narrative when, as though in a diary, he chronicles the circumstances attendant on the beginning of the Savior's public ministry, with four successive definite indications of time (1:29, 35, 43; 2:1). He lays special emphasis on Jesus' first miracles: "This beginning of signs Jesus did in Cana of Galilee" (2:11); "this again is the second sign that Jesus did, when he had come out of Judea into Galilee" (4:54). Finally, he refers repeatedly to the great religious and national festivals of the Jews for the purpose of indicating the exact historical sequence of events (2:13; 5:1; 6:4; 7:2; 10:22; 12:1; 13:1).

In a far higher degree than in the Synoptics, the whole narrative of the Fourth Gospel centers around the person of Christ. From his very opening sentences John turns his gaze to the inmost recesses of eternity, to the Divine Word at the side of the Father (1:1–18). He never tires of portraying the dignity and glory of the Eternal Word, who took up his abode among humans so that, while receiving the revelation of his divine majesty, they might also participate in the fullness of his grace and truth. As evidence of the deity of the Savior the author chronicles some of the great wonders by which Christ revealed his glory, but he is far more intent on leading his readers to a deeper understanding of Christ's divinity and majesty by a consideration of his words, discourses, and teaching and to impress upon their minds the far more glorious marvels of his divine love.

If we exclude the heretics mentioned by Irenaeus (*Against Heresies* 3.11.9) and Epiphanius (*Heresies* 50.3), the authenticity of the Fourth Gospel was scarcely ever seriously questioned until the end of the eighteenth century. In the titles, tables of contents, and signatures that are frequently added to the text of the separate Gospels, John is in every case and without the faintest indication of doubt named as the author of this Gospel. The earliest extant codex manuscripts, it is true, do not date back beyond the middle of the fourth century, but the perfect unanimity of all the codices indicates that the prototypes of these manuscripts, at a much earlier date, must have contained the same indications of authorship. Similar is the testimony of the Gospel translations, of which the Syrian, Coptic, and Old Latin extend back in their earliest forms to the second century.

The evidence given by the early ecclesiastical authors agrees with that of the above-mentioned sources. Dionysius of Alexandria (ca. 264), it is true, sought a different author for the Apocalypse, owing to the influence of the Chiliasts in Egypt; but he always took as undoubted that the apostle John was the author of the Fourth Gospel. Equally clear is the testimony of Origen (died ca. 254). He knew from church tradition that John was the last evangelist to compose his Gospel (Eusebius, *Ecclesiastical History* 7.25.6); and Origen's commentary on the Gospel of John is replete with his conviction of the apostolic origin of the work. Origen's teacher, Clement of Alexandria (died ca. 215), relates as the "tradition of the earliest elders" that the apostle John, the last of the evangelists, "filled with the Holy Spirit, had written a spiritual gospel" (Eusebius, *Ecclesiastical History* 6.14.7).

Of still greater importance is the testimony of Bishop Irenaeus of Lyons (died ca. 200), linked as he is with the apostolic era through his teacher Polycarp, the disciple of the apostle John. The native country of Irenaeus (Asia Minor) and the scene of his subsequent ministry (Gaul) render him a witness of the faith to both the eastern and the western churches. He cites in his writings at least one hundred verses from the Fourth Gospel, often with the remark, "as John, the disciple of the Lord, says." In speaking of the composition of the four Gospels, he says of the last: "Later John, the disciple of the Lord and the one who leaned against his chest, also put out a gospel while residing in Ephesus of Asia" (*Against Heresies* 3.1.2). It is clear that by "John, the disciple of the Lord," he means none other than the apostle John.

The same conviction concerning the authorship of the Fourth Gospel is expressed at greater length in the Roman church, about 150, by the writer of the Muratorian Fragment (lines 9–34). Bishop Theophilus of Antioch in Syria (before 181) also cites the beginning of the Fourth Gospel as the words of John (*Ad Autolycum* 2.22). Finally, according to the testimony of a Vatican manuscript, Papias of Hierapolis in Phrygia, an immediate disciple of the apostle John, included in his great exegetical work an account of the composition of the Gospel by John during which he had been employed as a scribe by the apostle. It is scarcely necessary to repeat that, in the passages referred to, Papias and the other ancient writers have in mind but one John, namely the apostle and evangelist, and not some other Elder John who is to be distinguished from the apostle.

The Gospel of John was composed in the last decade of the first century, or more precisely 96 or one of the succeeding years. The grounds for this opinion are briefly as follows: The Fourth Gospel was probably composed after the three Synoptics; it was written after the death of Peter, since the last chapter presupposes the death of the prince of the apostles; it was also written after the destruction of Jerusalem and the temple, for the evangelist seems to indicate that the end of the city and of the people as a nation has already come; 21:23 implies that John was already far advanced in years when he wrote the Gospel; those who denied the deity of Christ, the very point to which John devotes special attention throughout his Gospel, began to disseminate their heresy about the end of the first century; and finally, we have direct evidence concerning the date of composition. The Monarchian Prologue to the Fourth Gospel, probably written about 200 or a little later, says concerning the date of the appearance of the Gospel: "He [the apostle John] wrote this gospel in the province of Asia, after he had composed the Apocalypse on the Island of Patmos." The banishment of John to Patmos occurred in the last year of Domitian's reign (ca. 95). A few months before his death on September 18, 96, the emperor had discontinued the persecution of the Christians and recalled the exiles (Eusebius, *Ecclesiastical History* 3.20.5–7). This evidence indicates that the Gospel was composed in 96 or one of the years immediately following.

According to the Monarchian Prologue, the place of composition was the province of Asia. Still more precise is the statement of Irenaeus, who tells us that John wrote his Gospel "in Ephesus of Asia" (*Against Heresies* 3.1.2). All the other early references are in agreement with these statements. Hence the first readers of the Gospel were second-generation and third-generation Christians in Asia Minor. As there was no need of initiating them into the elements of the faith, John must have aimed rather at confirming them against the attacks of the opponents of the faith handed down by their parents.

Conclusion

The main purpose of this chapter has been to show that, on the basis of the Fourfold-Gospel Hypothesis, it is possible to discover a credible *Sitz im Leben* for the Gospel of Matthew when it is anchored in the period 30–44. Matthew's Gospel is the product of the earliest determination of the primitive church to preserve the teaching of its founder and to justify its separation from old Israel. On the other hand, the Gospel of Luke is the product of the crisis caused by the emergence of the Gentile churches alongside the primitive Jewish church; and they were churches that needed to develop their own interpretation of the Christian mission as a sign and proof of their full and equal status. It was the vital need to fuse together these two traditions—and the Gospels that symbolized them—into an unbreakable unity that led to the Gospel of Mark as the bridge between them and as the enabling document for Luke's Gospel to take its place as the second authentic witness to Jesus in the churches of both Peter and Paul. Finally, the Gospel of John, which almost all agree is subsequent to the Synoptics, supplements the earlier accounts by supplying information not already accessible in them.

The circumstances of the writing of the four Gospels and their relationships may be conveniently summarized as follows.

Stage 1

- The Holy Spirit descends upon the Jerusalem church on the day of Pentecost (30).
- The believers witness to Christ's life, death, and resurrection.
- The apostles realize the need for a written record of the min-

istry of Jesus to serve as a witness in their place wherever they cannot do so personally.

- The apostle Matthew is chosen to set down in a single commercial-length scroll the apostles' witness to the life, death, and resurrection of Christ.
- The "Gospel according to Matthew" is published before the apostles separate under the persecution of Herod Agrippa I in 42.

Stage 2

- Paul evangelizes the Gentiles and encounters problems peculiar to the pagan environment of his converts.
- During his detention in Caesarea, Paul prompts Luke to provide a fuller elucidation of Jesus' ministry and of the place of the Gentiles in the kingdom of God.
- Luke produces a "Gentile edition" of the Gospel of Matthew in 58–60.
- The publication of the "Gospel according to Luke" is withheld until apostolic approbation can guarantee its truthfulness and accuracy.

Stage 3

- During his Roman detention in 60–62, Paul asks Peter to check and authorize Luke's Gospel so that it can be published for use in the Gentile churches.
- Peter's response is given in a series of lectures before a distinguished Roman audience.
- These lectures are recorded by John Mark, Peter's secretary, and are issued privately in written form to members of the Roman church at their request.
- Luke's text is published in 62 as the authoritative "Gentile edition" of the Gospel.

- After the death of Peter in 66/67, the "Gospel according to Mark" is published, Mark himself adding the last twelve verses to provide a fitting conclusion to Peter's reminiscences.

Stage 4

- The Gospel of John is published in Ephesus in 96 as the indispensable supplement to the other Gospel accounts.

Postscript

THE UNHESITATING SUPPORT by the church fathers for the historicity and authorship of the four Gospels can no longer be doubted, nor can it be questioned that the earliest church believed that the apostle Matthew was the first to write a Gospel. Moreover, the internal evidence, far from backing the priority of Mark, equally supports the priority of Matthew over Mark. It is also plain that not only apostles, but also "apostolic men," were involved in the composition of the Gospels, which is an acknowledgment of the tradition that two of the Gospels were ascribed to the apostles Matthew and John; the other two, Mark and Luke, were ascribed to "apostolic men" or associates of the apostles.

Nevertheless, the tradition of Matthean priority is today rejected by most Gospel critics—a situation all the more inexplicable in view of the fact that the vast amount of research done on the synoptic problem over the past two hundred years has utterly failed to bring about a satisfying consensus. Markan priorists unfortunately see no reason to dialogue seriously with the relatively few supporters of the ancient tradition that the apostle Matthew wrote the first Gospel.

Could it not be, however, that the Markan priorists are wrong? Ought we to conclude that the earliest authorities were in error in affirming the apostolic authorship and full historicity of the four Gospels? There is enough uncertainty, doubt, and contradiction to require those who rely on Markan priority to listen patiently to those who propose another way of interpreting the literary, historical, and patristic evidence that satisfies the most rigorous requirements of scholarship.

In other words, it is high time to rethink the data; and, in fact, an important attempt to start such a dialogue took place at Southeastern Seminary's Symposium on New Testament Studies in April 2000.[1] That dialogue must now be taken up again in earnest. In particular, the relationship between historicity and apostolicity will have to be reexamined because discussion of this relationship seems to have been suspended with the acquiescence of the scholarly guild to Markan priority. If the Fourfold-Gospel Hypothesis is found to be the correct source-critical theory, then there will be no problem either in the apostle Matthew being the author of his Gospel or in Peter and Paul authenticating the Gospels of Mark and Luke, since it proves that Matthew and Luke were written before Mark, which itself is dated about 62, thus permitting all three Synoptic Gospels to have been written during the life span of Matthew and the "apostolic men."

A large number of books and articles dealing with the synoptic problem and the weaknesses of the Markan priority hypothesis has appeared in recent years, and the following bibliography records some of the more important titles. The search for truth requires the testing of the Fourfold-Gospel Hypothesis with the same thoroughness that has called into question the credibility of Markan priority.

---

1. These papers have now been published in D. R. Beck and D. A. Black (eds.), *Rethinking the Synoptic Problem* (Grand Rapids: Baker, 2001).

Bibliography

Abbott, Edwin A. *The Corrections of Mark Adopted by Matthew and Luke.* London: Black, 1901.

——. *The Fourfold Gospel.* Cambridge: Cambridge University Press, 1913.

Abbott, Edwin A., and W. G. Rushbrooke. *The Common Tradition of the Synoptic Gospels in the Text of the Revised Version.* London: Macmillan, 1884.

Abogunrin, Samuel O. "The Synoptic Gospel Debate: A Reexamination in an African Context." *African Journal of Biblical Studies* 2 (1987): 25–51.

Aland, Kurt (ed.). *Synopsis of the Four Gospels: Greek-English Edition of the Synopsis Quattuor Evangeliorum.* Stuttgart: German Bible Society, 1993.

——. *Synopsis Quattuor Evangeliorum.* 3d ed. Stuttgart: Württembergische Bibelanstalt, 1965.

Allison, Dale C., Jr. *The Jesus Tradition in Q.* Harrisburg, Pa.: Trinity, 1997.

Argyle, A. W. "Evidence for the View That St. Luke Used St. Matthew's Gospel." *Journal of Biblical Literature* 83 (1964): 390–96.

Barr, Allan. *A Diagram of Synoptic Relationships.* 2d ed. Edinburgh: Clark, 1995.

Barrett, C. K. "Q: A Re-examination." *Expository Times* 54 (1942–43): 320–23.

Bauckham, Richard (ed.). *The Gospels for All Christians: Rethinking the Gospel Audiences.* Grand Rapids: Eerdmans, 1998.

Bea, Augustin. *The Study of the Synoptic Gospels.* New York: Harper & Row, 1964.

Beck, David R., and David Alan Black. *Rethinking the Synoptic Problem.* Grand Rapids: Baker, 2001.

Bellinzoni, Arthur J., Jr., Joseph B. Tyson, and William O. Walker Jr. (eds.). *The Two-Source Hypothesis: A Critical Appraisal.* Macon, Ga.: Mercer University Press, 1985.

Black, David Alan. "Conjectural Emendations in the Gospel of Matthew." *Novum Testamentum* 31 (1989): 1–15.

———. "Discourse Analysis, Synoptic Criticism, and the Problem of Markan Grammar: Some Methodological Considerations." Pages 89–98 in *Linguistics and New Testament Interpretation.* Edited by David Alan Black. Nashville: Broadman & Holman, 1992.

———. "El Grupo de Juan: Helenismo y Gnosis." Pages 303–23 in *Origenes del Cristianismo.* Edited by A. Piñero. Cordoba: el Almendro, 1991.

———. "Jesus on Anger: The Text of Matthew 5:22a Revisited." *Novum Testamentum* 30 (1988): 1–8.

———. "Some Dissenting Notes on R. Stein's *The Synoptic Problem* and Markan 'Errors.'" *Filología Neotestamentaria* 1 (1988): 95–101.

———. "The Text of Mark 6:20." *New Testament Studies* 34 (1988): 141–45.

Blomberg, Craig L. *Jesus and the Gospels: An Introduction and Survey.* Nashville: Broadman & Holman, 1997.

Boismard, M. E. "Two-Source Hypothesis." Pages 679–82 in vol. 6 of *The Anchor Bible Dictionary.* Edited by David Noel Freedman. New York: Doubleday, 1992.

———. "The Two-Source Theory at an Impasse." *New Testament Studies* 26 (1980): 1–17.

Bradby, E. L. "In Defense of Q." *Expository Times* 68 (1956–57): 315–18.

Buckley, E. L. *An Introduction to the Synoptic Problem.* London: Arnold, 1912.

Burkitt, F. C. *The Gospel History and Its Transmission.* 2d ed. Edinburgh: Clark, 1907.

Burridge, Richard A. *Four Gospels, One Jesus?* Grand Rapids: Eerdmans, 1994.

Butler, B. C. *The Originality of St. Matthew: A Critique of the Two-Document Hypothesis.* Cambridge: Cambridge University Press, 1951.

———. "St. Luke's Debt to St. Matthew." *Harvard Theological Review* 32 (1939): 237–308.

———. "St. Paul's Knowledge and Use of St. Matthew." *Downside Review* 60 (1948): 363–83.

Carrington, P. *According to Mark.* Cambridge: Cambridge University Press, 1960.

Casey, Maurice. *Aramaic Sources of Mark's Gospel.* Society for New Testament Studies Monograph Series 102. Cambridge: Cambridge University Press, 1998.

Catchpole, David R. "The Beginning of Q: A Proposal." *New Testament Studies* 38 (1992): 205–21.

Chapman, John. *John the Presbyter.* Oxford: Oxford University Press, 1911.

———. *Matthew, Mark and Luke: A Study in the Order and Interrelation of the Synoptic Gospels.* London: Longmans & Green, 1937.

Cope, O. Lamar. *Matthew: A Scribe Trained for the Kingdom of Heaven.* Catholic Biblical Quarterly Monograph Series 5. Washington, D.C.: Catholic Biblical Association of America, 1976.

Crompton, R. H. *The Synoptic Problem and a New Solution.* Edinburgh: Clark, 1928.

Davies, W. D., and Dale C. Allison Jr. *The Gospel according to Saint Matthew.* Vol. 1. Edinburgh: Clark, 1988.

Downing, F. G. "Compositional Conventions and the Synoptic Problem." *Journal of Biblical Literature* 107 (1988): 69–85.

———. "A Paradigm Perplex: Luke, Matthew and Mark." *New Testament Studies* 38 (1992): 15–36.

———. "Towards the Rehabilitation of Q." *New Testament Studies* 11 (1964–65): 169–81.

Dunderberg, Ismo. "Q and the Beginning of Mark." *New Testament Studies* 41 (1995): 501–11.

Dungan, David L. "A Griesbachian Perspective on the Argument from Order." Pages 67–74 in *Synoptic Studies: The Ampleforth Conferences of 1982 and 1983.* Edited by C. M. Tuckett. Journal for the Study of the New Testament Supplement 7. Sheffield: JSOT Press, 1984.

———. *A History of the Synoptic Problem: The Canon, the Text, the Composition and the Interpretation of the Gospels.* New York: Doubleday, 1999.

———. "Mark—The Abridgement of Matthew and Luke." Pages 51–97 in vol. 1 of *Jesus and Man's Hope.* Edited by David G. Buttrick. Pittsburgh: Pittsburgh Theological Seminary, 1970.

———. "The Purpose and Provenance of the Gospel of Mark according to the Two-Gospel (Owen-Griesbach) Hypothesis." Pages 411–40 in *New Synoptic Studies: The Cambridge Gospel Conference and Beyond.* Edited by William R. Farmer. Macon, Ga.: Mercer University Press, 1983.

———. *The Sayings of Jesus in the Churches of Paul.* Philadelphia: Fortress, 1971.

———. "Synopses of the Future." Pages 317–47 in *The Interrelations of the Gospels.* Edited by David L. Dungan. Bibliotheca ephemeridum theologicarum lovaniensium 95. Leuven: Louvain University Press, 1990.

———. "Two-Gospel Hypothesis." Pages 671–79 in vol. 6 of *The Anchor Bible Dictionary.* Edited by David Noel Freedman. New York: Doubleday, 1992.

Dungan, David L. (ed.). *The Interrelations of the Gospels.* Bibliotheca ephemeridum theologicarum lovaniensium 95. Leuven: Louvain University Press, 1990.

Dungan, David L., and John S. Kloppenborg. "The Synoptic Problem: How Did We Get Our Gospels?" Pages 1231–40 in *The International Bible Commentary: A Catholic and Ecumenical Commentary for the Twenty-First Century.* Edited by William R. Farmer. Collegeville: Liturgical Press, 1998.

Elliott, J. K. "The Relevance of Textual Criticism to the Synoptic Problem." Pages 348–59 in *The Interrelations of the Gospels.* Edited by David L. Dungan. Bibliotheca ephemeridum theologicarum lovaniensium 95. Leuven: Louvain University Press, 1990.

Ellis, E. E. "Gospels Criticism: A Perspective on the State of the Art." Pages 26–52 in *The Gospel and the Gospels.* Edited by P. Stuhlmacher. Grand Rapids: Eerdmans, 1983.

———. *The Making of the New Testament Documents.* Leiden: Brill, 1999.

———. "The Synoptic Gospels and History." Pages 53–56 in *Authenticating the Activities of Jesus.* Edited by Bruce Chilton and Craig A. Evans. Leiden: Brill, 1999.

Farmer, William R. "Certain Results Reached by Sir John C. Hawkins and C. F. Burney Which Make More Sense If Luke Knew Matthew, and Mark Knew Matthew and Luke." Pages 75–98 in *Synoptic Studies: The Ampleforth Conferences of 1982 and 1983.* Edited by C. M. Tuckett. Journal for the Study of the New Testament Supplement 7. Sheffield: JSOT Press, 1984.

——. "A Fresh Approach to Q." Pages 39–50 in *Christianity, Judaism, and Other Greco-Roman Cults*. Edited by Jacob Neusner. Leiden: Brill, 1975.

——. *The Gospel of Jesus: The Pastoral Relevance of the Synoptic Problem*. Louisville: Westminster/John Knox, 1994.

——. *Jesus and the Gospel: Tradition, Scripture, and Canon*. Philadelphia: Fortress, 1982.

——. *The Last Twelve Verses of Mark*. Cambridge: Cambridge University Press, 1974.

——. "The Present State of the Synoptic Problem." Pages 11–36 in *Literary Studies in Luke–Acts: Essays in Honor of Joseph B. Tyson*. Macon, Ga.: Mercer University Press, 1998.

——. "Reply to Michael Goulder." Pages 105–9 in *Synoptic Studies: The Ampleforth Conferences of 1982 and 1983*. Edited by C. M. Tuckett. Journal for the Study of the New Testament Supplement 7. Sheffield: JSOT Press, 1984.

——. "A Response to Joseph Fitzmyer's Defense of the Two Document Hypothesis." Pages 501–23 in *New Synoptic Studies: The Cambridge Gospel Conference and Beyond*. Edited by William R. Farmer. Macon, Ga.: Mercer University Press, 1983.

——. "The Statement of the Hypothesis." Pages 125–56 in *The Interrelations of the Gospels*. Edited by David L. Dungan. Bibliotheca ephemeridum theologicarum lovaniensium 95. Leuven: Louvain University Press, 1990.

——. *The Synoptic Problem: A Critical Analysis*. New York: Macmillan, 1964.

Farmer, William R. (ed.). *New Synoptic Studies: The Cambridge Gospel Conference and Beyond*. Macon, Ga.: Mercer University Press, 1983.

Farrer, A. M. *A Study in St Mark*. Westminster: Dacre, 1951.

Farrer, M. "On Dispensing with Q." Pages 55–88 in *Studies in the Gospels: Essays in Memory of R. H. Lightfoot*. Edited by D. E. Nineham. Oxford: Blackwell, 1955.

Fee, Gordon D. "Modern Text Criticism and the Synoptic Problem." Pages 154–69 in *J. J. Griesbach: Synoptic and Text-Critical Studies, 1776–1976*. Edited by Bernard Orchard and Thomas R. W. Longstaff. Society for New Testament Studies Monograph Series 34. Cambridge: Cambridge University Press, 1978.

———. "A Text-Critical Look at the Synoptic Problem." *Novum Testamentum* 22 (1980): 12–28.

Fitzmyer, Joseph A. "The Priority of Mark and the 'Q' Source in Luke." Pages 131–70 in vol. 1 of *Jesus and Man's Hope*. Edited by David G. Buttrick. Pittsburgh: Pittsburgh Theological Seminary, 1970.

Goodacre, Mark S. "Beyond the Q Impasse or Down a Blind Alley?" *Journal for the Study of the New Testament* 76 (1999): 33–52.

———. "Fatigue in the Synoptics." *New Testament Studies* 44 (1998): 45–58.

———. *Goulder and the Gospels: An Examination of a New Paradigm*. Journal for the Study of the New Testament Supplement 133. Sheffield: Academic Press, 1996.

Goulder, Michael D. "Is Q a Juggernaut?" *Journal of Biblical Literature* 115 (1996): 667–81.

———. *Luke: A New Paradigm*. Journal for the Study of the New Testament Supplement 20. Sheffield: Academic Press, 1989.

———. *Midrash and Lection in Matthew*. London: SPCK, 1974.

———. "On Putting Q to the Test." *New Testament Studies* 24 (1978): 218–34.

———. "The Order of a Crank." Pages 111–30 in *Synoptic Studies: The Ampleforth Conferences of 1982 and 1983*. Edited by C. M. Tuckett. Journal for the Study of the New Testament Supplement 7. Sheffield: JSOT Press, 1984.

———. "Some Observations on Professor Farmer's 'Certain Results. . . .'" Pages 99–104 in *Synoptic Studies: The Ampleforth Conferences of 1982 and 1983.* Edited by C. M. Tuckett. Journal for the Study of the New Testament Supplement 7. Sheffield: JSOT Press, 1984.

Grant, Frederick C. *The Gospels: Their Origin and Their Growth.* New York: Harper & Row, 1957.

Greeven, Heinrich. "The Gospel Synopsis from 1776 to the Present Day." Pages 22–49 in *J. J. Griesbach: Synoptic and Text-Critical Studies, 1776–1976.* Edited by Bernard Orchard and Thomas R. W. Longstaff. Society for New Testament Studies Monograph Series 34. Cambridge: Cambridge University Press, 1978.

Griesbach, Johan Jakob. "A Demonstration That Mark Was Written after Matthew and Luke." Translated by Bernard Orchard. Pages 103–35 in *J. J. Griesbach: Synoptic and Text-Critical Studies, 1776–1976.* Edited by Bernard Orchard and Thomas R. W. Longstaff. Society for New Testament Studies Monograph Series 34. Cambridge: Cambridge University Press, 1978.

Gundry, Robert H. *Mark: A Commentary on His Apology for the Cross.* Grand Rapids: Eerdmans, 1993.

———. *Matthew: A Commentary on His Handbook for a Mixed Church under Persecution.* 2d ed. Grand Rapids: Eerdmans, 1994.

Guy, Harold A. *The Origin of the Gospel of Mark.* London: Hodder & Stoughton, 1954.

Hawkins, John C. *Horae Synopticae: Contributions to the Study of the Synoptic Problem.* 2d ed. Oxford: Clarendon, 1909 (originally 1899).

Head, Peter M. *Christology and the Synoptic Problem: An Argument for Markan Priority.* Society for New Testament Studies Monograph Series 94. Cambridge: Cambridge University Press, 1997.

Hengel, Martin. *Studies in the Gospel of Mark.* Minneapolis: Fortress, 1985.

Hobbs, Edward C. "A Quarter-Century Without 'Q.'" *Perkins Journal* (Summer 1980): 10–19.

Honoré, A. M. "A Statistical Study of the Synoptic Problem." *Novum Testamentum* 10 (1968): 95–147.

Jacobson, Arland D. "The Literary Unity of Q." *Journal of Biblical Literature* 101 (1982): 365–89.

Jameson, G. *The Origin of the Synoptic Gospels: A Revision of the Synoptic Problem.* Oxford: Basil Blackwell, 1922.

Johnson, Sherman E. *The Griesbach Hypothesis and Redaction Criticism.* Society of Biblical Literature Monograph Series 41. Atlanta: Scholars Press, 1991.

Kilpatrick, G. D. *The Origins of the Gospel According to St. Matthew.* Oxford: Clarendon, 1946.

Kloppenborg, John S. *Excavating Q: The History and Setting of the Sayings Gospel.* Minneapolis: Fortress, 2000.

———. *The Formation of Q: Trajectories in Ancient Wisdom Collections.* Philadelphia: Fortress, 1987.

———. *Q Parallels: Synopsis, Critical Notes, and Concordance.* Sonoma, Calif.: Polebridge, 1988.

———. "The Theological Stakes in the Synoptic Problem." Pages 93–120 in vol. 1 of *The Four Gospels, 1992.* Edited by F. Van Segbroeck et al. Bibliotheca ephemeridum theologicarum lovaniensium 100. Leuven: Louvain University Press, 1992.

Kloppenborg, John S. (ed.). *Conflict and Invention: Literary, Rhetorical, and Social Studies on the Sayings Gospel Q.* Valley Forge, Pa.: Trinity, 1995.

———. *The Shape of Q: Signal Essays on the Sayings Gospel.* Minneapolis: Fortress, 1994.

Koester, Helmut. *Ancient Christian Gospels: Their History and Development.* Philadelphia: Trinity, 1990.

———. "History and Development of Mark's Gospel." Pages 35–57 in *Colloquy on New Testament Studies: A Time for Reappraisal and Fresh Approaches.* Edited by Bruce C. Corley. Macon, Ga.: Mercer University Press, 1983.

Kümmel, W. G. *Introduction to the New Testament.* Nashville: Abingdon, 1965.

Kürzinger, J. "Das Papiaszeugnis und die Erstgestalt des Matthäusevangeliums." *Biblische Zeitschrift* 4 (1960): 19–38.

———. "Irenäus und sein Zeugnis zur Sprache des Matthäusevangeliums." *New Testament Studies* 10 (1963): 108–15.

———. *Papias von Hierapolis und die Evangelien des Neuen Testaments.* Regensburg: Pustet, 1983.

Lindsey, Robert Lisle. *A Hebrew Translation of the Gospel of Mark: Greek-Hebrew Diglot with English Introduction.* Jerusalem: Dugith, 1973.

Linnemann, Eta. *Is There a Synoptic Problem?* Translated by Robert Yarbrough. Grand Rapids: Baker, 1992.

Longstaff, Thomas R. W. *Evidence of Conflation in Mark? A Study in the Synoptic Problem.* Society of Biblical Literature Dissertation Series 26. Missoula, Mont.: Scholars Press, 1977.

Longstaff, Thomas R. W., and Page A. Thomas. *The Synoptic Problem: A Bibliography, 1716–1988.* Macon, Ga.: Mercer University Press, 1988.

Lührmann, Dieter. "The Gospel of Mark and the Sayings Collection Q." *Journal of Biblical Literature* 108 (1989): 51–71.

Massaux, Édouard. *Influence of the Gospel of Saint Matthew on Christian Literature before Saint Irenaeus.* 3 vols. Translated by Norman J. Belval and Suzanne Hecht. Edited by Arthur J. Bellinzoni Jr. New Gospel Studies 5. Macon, Ga.: Mercer University Press, 1990 (originally 1950).

Mattila, Sharon L. "A Problem Still Clouded: Yet Again–Statistics and 'Q.' " *Novum Testamentum* 37 (1994): 105–29.

McKnight, Scot. *Interpreting the Synoptic Gospels.* Grand Rapids: Baker, 1988.

McNicol, Allan J., David L. Dungan, and David B. Peabody (eds.). *Beyond the Q Impasse: Luke's Use of Matthew.* Valley Forge, Pa.: Trinity, 1996.

Menzies, Allan. *The Earliest Gospel: A Historical Study of the Gospel according to Mark.* London: Macmillan, 1901.

Metzger, Bruce M. *The Text of the New Testament.* Oxford: Oxford University Press, 1968.

Neirynck, Frans. "Introduction: The Two-Source Hypothesis." Pages 3–22 in *The Interrelations of the Gospels.* Edited by David L. Dungan. Bibliotheca ephemeridum theologicarum lovaniensium 95. Leuven: Louvain University Press, 1990.

———. "The Minor Agreements and Q." Pages 49–72 in *The Gospel behind the Gospels: Current Studies on Q.* Edited by Ronald A. Piper. Novum Testamentum Supplement 75. Leiden: Brill, 1995.

———. *The Minor Agreements of Matthew and Luke against Mark with a Cumulative List.* Bibliotheca ephemeridum theologicarum lovaniensium 37. Leuven: Louvain University Press, 1974.

———. "Synoptic Problem." Pages 845–48 in *The Interpreter's Dictionary of the Bible: Supplement Volume.* Edited by Keith Crim. Nashville: Abingdon, 1976.

———. "Synoptic Problem." Pages 587–95 in *The New Jerome Biblical Commentary.* Edited by Raymond Brown et al. Englewood Cliffs, N.J.: Prentice Hall, 1990.

Neirynck, Frans, and J. Verhayden. *The Gospel of Matthew and the Sayings Source Q: A Cumulative Bibliography, 1950–1995.* 2 vols. Bibliotheca ephemeridum theologicarum lovaniensium 105. Leuven: Louvain University Press, 1998.

Neville, David J. *Arguments from Order in Synoptic Source Criticism: A History and Critique.* New Gospel Studies 7. Macon, Ga.: Mercer University Press, 1994.

New, David S. *Old Testament Quotations in the Synoptic Gospels and the Two-Document Hypothesis.* Atlanta: Scholars Press, 1993.

Nickle, Keith F. *The Synoptic Gospels: Conflict and Consensus*. Atlanta: John Knox, 1980.

Orchard, Bernard. "*Dei Verbum* and the Synoptic Gospels." *Downside Review* 108 (1990): 199–214.

———. "The Ellipsis Between Galatians 2:3 and 2:4." *Biblica* 54 (1973): 469–81.

———. *The Evolution of the Gospels*. London: Ealing Abbey, n.d.

———. "The Formation of the Synoptic Gospels." *Downside Review* 106 (1988): 1–16.

———. "J. A. T. Robinson and the Synoptic Problem." *New Testament Studies* 22 (1976): 346–52.

———. "The Making and Publication of Mark's Gospel—An Historical Investigation." *Annales Theologici* 7 (1993): 369–93.

———. *Matthew, Luke and Mark*. Manchester: Koinonia, 1976.

———. "A New Solution of the Galatians Problem." *Bulletin of the John Rylands Library* 28 (1944): 154–74.

———. "A Note on the Meaning of Galatians 2:3–5." *Journal of Theological Studies* 43 (1942): 173–77.

———. "Once Again: The Ellipsis Between Galatians 2:3 and 2:4." *Biblica* 57 (1976): 254–55.

———. "The Problem of Acts and Galatians." *Catholic Biblical Quarterly* 7 (1945): 377–97.

———. "The Solution of the Synoptic Problem." *Scripture Bulletin* 18 (1987).

———. "Some Reflections on the Relationship of Luke to Matthew." Pages 33–46 in *Jesus, the Gospels, and the Church*. Edited by E. P. Sanders. Macon, Ga.: Mercer University Press, 1987.

———. *A Synopsis of the Four Gospels in English*. Macon, Ga.: Mercer University Press/Edinburgh: Clark, 1982.

———. *A Synopsis of the Four Gospels in Greek*. Macon, Ga.: Mercer University Press/Edinburgh: Clark, 1983.

———. "Thessalonians and the Synoptic Gospels." *Biblica* 19 (1938): 19–42.

———. "The Two-Document Hypothesis or, Some Thoughts on the Revival of the Griesbach Hypothesis." *Downside Review* 98 (1980): 267–79.

———. *The Two-Gospel Hypothesis.* London: Ealing Abbey, 1989.

Orchard, Bernard (ed.). *A Catholic Commentary on Holy Scripture.* London, 1953.

Orchard, Bernard, and Thomas R. W. Longstaff (eds.). *J. J. Griesbach: Synoptic and Text-Critical Studies, 1776–1976.* Society for New Testament Studies Monograph Series 34. Cambridge: Cambridge University Press, 1978.

Orchard, Bernard, and Harold Riley. *The Order of the Synoptics: Why Three Synoptic Gospels?* Macon, Ga.: Mercer University Press, 1987.

Orton, David E. (ed.). *The Synoptic Problem and Q: Selected Studies from Novum Testamentum.* Leiden: Brill, 1999.

Overman, J. Andrew. *Matthew's Gospel and Formative Judaism: The Social World of the Matthean Community.* Minneapolis: Fortress, 1990.

Owen, Henry. *Observations on the Four Gospels.* London: 1764.

Palmer, N. H. "Lachmann's Argument." New Testament Studies 13 (1966–67): 368–78.

Parker, David C. *The Living Text of the Gospels.* Cambridge: Cambridge University Press, 1997.

Parker, Pierson. *The Gospel before Mark.* Chicago: University of Chicago Press, 1953.

———. "The Posteriority of Mark." Pages 65–142 in *New Synoptic Studies: The Cambridge Gospel Conference and Beyond.* Edited by William R. Farmer. Macon, Ga.: Mercer University Press, 1983.

———. "A Second Look at *The Gospel before Mark.*" *Journal of Biblical Literature* 100 (1980): 389–413.

Patzia, Arthur G. *The Making of the New Testament: Origin, Collection, Text and Canon.* Downers Grove, Ill.: InterVarsity, 1995.

Peabody, David. "Augustine and the Augustinian Hypothesis: A Reexamination of Augustine's Thought in *De consensu evangelistarum.*" Pages 37–64 in *New Synoptic Studies: The Cambridge Gospel Conference and Beyond.* Edited by William R. Farmer. Macon, Ga.: Mercer University Press, 1983.

———. "The Late Secondary Redaction of Mark's Gospel and the Griesbach Hypothesis: A Response to Helmut Koester." Pages 87–132 in *Colloquy on New Testament Studies: A Time for Reappraisal and Fresh Approaches.* Edited by Bruce C. Corley. Macon, Ga.: Mercer University Press, 1983.

———. *Mark as Composer.* New Gospel Studies 1. Macon, Ga.: Mercer University Press, 1987.

Petrie, Stewart "'Q' Is Only What You Make It." *Novum Testamentum* 3 (1959): 28–33.

Reddish, M. G. *An Introduction to the Gospels.* Nashville: Abingdon, 1997.

Reicke, Bo. "Griesbach's Answer to the Synoptic Question." Pages 50–67 and 198–200 in *J. J. Griesbach: Synoptic and Text-Critical Studies, 1776–1976.* Edited by Bernard Orchard and Thomas R. W. Longstaff. Society for New Testament Studies Monograph Series 34. Cambridge: Cambridge University Press, 1978.

———. "The History of the Synoptic Discussion." Pages 291–316 in *The Interrelations of the Gospels.* Edited by David L. Dungan. Bibliotheca ephemeridum theologicarum lovaniensium 95. Leuven: Louvain University Press, 1990.

———. "Introduction to Griesbach's *Commentatio.*" Pages 68–73 in *J. J. Griesbach: Synoptic and Text-Critical Studies, 1776–1976.* Edited by Bernard Orchard and Thomas R. W. Longstaff. Society for New Testament Studies Monograph Series 34. Cambridge: Cambridge University Press, 1978.

———. *The Roots of the Synoptic Gospels.* Philadelphia: Fortress, 1986.

Richards, E. Randolph. *The Secretary in the Letters of Paul.* Tübingen: Mohr/Siebeck, 1991.

Riley, Harold. *The First Gospel.* Macon, Ga.: Mercer University Press, 1992.

———. *The Making of Mark: An Exploration.* Macon, Ga.: Mercer University Press, 1989.

———. *Preface to Luke.* Macon, Ga.: Mercer University Press, 1993.

Rist, John M. *On the Independence of Matthew and Mark.* Society for New Testament Studies Monograph Series 32. Cambridge: Cambridge University Press, 1978.

Robinson, John A. T. *Redating the New Testament.* London: SCM, 1976.

Rosché, T. R. "The Words of Jesus and the Future of the 'Q' Hypothesis." *Journal of Biblical Literature* 79 (1960): 210–20.

Sanday, William (ed.). *Studies in the Synoptic Problem.* Oxford: Clarendon, 1911.

Sanders, E. P. "The Argument from Order and the Relationship between Matthew and Luke." *New Testament Studies* 15 (1968–69): 249–61.

———. "The Overlaps of Mark and Q and the Synoptic Problem." *New Testament Studies* 19 (1972–73): 453–65.

———. *The Tendencies of the Synoptic Tradition.* Society for New Testament Studies Monograph Series 9. Cambridge: Cambridge University Press, 1969.

Sanders, E. P., and Margaret Davies. *Studying the Synoptic Gospels.* London: SCM, 1989.

Sherwin-White, A. N. *Roman Society and Roman Law in the New Testament.* Oxford: Oxford University Press, 1963.

Simpson, R. T. "The Major Agreements of Matthew and Luke against Mark." *New Testament Studies* 12 (1965–66): 273–84.

Smith, Robinson. *The Solution of the Synoptic Problem: Sources, Sequences and Dates of the Gospels and Epistles, and the Consequent Life of Christ.* London: Watts, 1922.

Stanton, Graham N. *A Gospel for a New People: Studies in Matthew.* Louisville: Westminster/John Knox, 1992.

———. *The Gospels and Jesus.* Oxford: Oxford University Press, 1989.

Stein, Robert H. *Gospels and Tradition: Studies on Redaction Criticism of the Synoptic Gospels.* Grand Rapids: Baker, 1991.

———. "The Matthew–Luke Agreements against Mark: Insight from John." *Catholic Biblical Quarterly* 54 (1992): 482–502.

———. "Synoptic Problem." Pages 784–92 in *Dictionary of Jesus and the Gospels.* Edited by Joel B. Green, Scot McKnight, and I. Howard Marshall. Downers Grove, Ill.: InterVarsity, 1992.

———. *The Synoptic Problem: An Introduction.* Grand Rapids: Baker, 1987.

Stoldt, Hans-Herbert. *History and Criticism of the Markan Hypothesis.* Macon, Ga.: Mercer University Press, 1980.

Stonehouse, Ned B. *Origins of the Synoptic Gospels: Some Basic Questions.* Grand Rapids: Baker, 1979 (originally 1963).

Streeter, B. H. *The Four Gospels: A Study of Origins.* London: Macmillan, 1924.

———. "St. Mark's Knowledge and Use of Q." Pages 165–83 in *Studies in the Synoptic Problem.* Edited by William Sanday. Oxford: Clarendon, 1911.

Styler, G. M. "The Priority of Mark." Pages 223–32 in *The Birth of the New Testament.* By C. F. D. Moule. London: Black, 1962.

Taylor, R. O. P. *The Groundwork of the Gospels.* Oxford: Oxford University Press, 1946.

Taylor, Vincent. *The Formation of the Gospel Tradition.* 2d ed. London: Macmillan, 1935.

Throckmorton, Burton H., Jr. (ed.). *Gospel Parallels: A Comparison of the Synoptic Gospels, with Alternative Readings from the Manuscripts and Noncanonical Parallels.* 5th ed. Nashville: Nelson, 1992.

Tuckett, C. M. "Arguments from Order: Definition and Evaluation." Pages 197–219 in *Synoptic Studies: The Ampleforth Con-*

ferences of 1982 and 1983. Edited by C. M. Tuckett. Journal for the Study of the New Testament Supplement 7. Sheffield: JSOT Press, 1984.

——. "The Beatitudes: A Source-Critical Study, with a Reply by M. D. Goulder." *Novum Testamentum* 25 (1983): 193–216.

——. "The Existence of Q." Pages 19–47 in *The Gospel behind the Gospels: Current Studies on Q*. Edited by Ronald A. Piper. Novum Testamentum Supplement 75. Leiden: Brill, 1995.

——. "Jesus and the Gospels." Pages 71–86 in vol. 8 of *The New Interpreter's Bible*. Nashville: Abingdon, 1995.

——. "On the Relationship between Matthew and Luke." *New Testament Studies* 30 (1984): 130–42.

——. *Q and the History of Early Christianity: Studies on Q*. Edinburgh: Clark, 1996.

——. *The Revival of the Griesbach Hypothesis: An Analysis and Appraisal*. Society for New Testament Studies Monograph Series 44. Cambridge: Cambridge University Press, 1983.

——. "Synoptic Problem." Pages 263–70 in vol. 6 of *The Anchor Bible Dictionary*. Edited by David Noel Freedman. New York: Doubleday, 1992.

Tuckett, C. M. (ed.). *The Messianic Secret*. Philadelphia: Fortress, 1983.

——. *Synoptic Studies: The Ampleforth Conferences of 1982 and 1983*. Journal for the Study of the New Testament Supplement 7. Sheffield: JSOT Press, 1984.

Turner, E. G. *Greek Papyri*. Oxford: Clarendon, 1980.

Tyson, Joseph B. *The New Testament and Early Christianity*. New York: Macmillan, 1984.

——. "The Two-Source Hypothesis: A Critical Appraisal." Pages 437–52 in *The Two-Source Hypothesis: A Critical Appraisal*. Edited by Arthur J. Bellinzoni Jr., Joseph B. Tyson, and William O. Walker Jr. Macon, Ga.: Mercer University Press, 1985.

Vassiliadis, Petros. "The Nature and Extent of the Q-Document." *Novum Testamentum* 20 (1978): 49–73.

Walker, William O., Jr. (ed.). *The Relationship among the Gospels: An Interdisciplinary Dialogue.* San Antonio, Tex.: Trinity University Press, 1978.

Watson, Francis. *Text and Truth: Redefining Biblical Theology.* Grand Rapids: Eerdmans, 1997.

Weeden, Theodore J. *Mark: Traditions in Conflict.* Philadelphia: Fortress, 1971.

Wenham, John. *Redating Matthew, Mark and Luke: A Fresh Assault on the Synoptic Problem.* Downers Grove, Ill.: InterVarsity, 1992.

Wilder, T. L. "Pseudonymity and the New Testament." Pages 293–332 in *Interpreting the New Testament.* Edited by David Alan Black and David S. Dockery. Nashville: Broadman & Holman, 2001.

Wood, H. G. "The Priority of Mark." *Expository Times* 65 (1953–54): 17–19.

Index

Achaia 29, 39
Acts 15–23, 38, 66, 76, 78
Against Heresies. See Irenaeus.
Against Marcion. See Tertullian.
Agreements, minor 56, 57
Agrippa I, Herod 20, 74, 81, 91
Alexandria, church at 30, 39, 40,
  85
Anti-Marcionite Prologue 39
Antioch 21–22, 54
Apocryphal Gospels 37
Apostles
  Authority of 8, 35, 69–70
  Inspiration of 35
  Work of 18–33, 35
Aramaic 50
Asia Minor 29, 38, 42, 46, 88, 89
Asia, Province of. *See* Asia Minor.
Augustine of Hippo 42, 85

Barnabas 21, 22, 25
Beatitudes 51
Bethany, anointing in 83
Bios literature 14, 73
Birth of Christ 17, 23–24, 27, 53,
  79

Caesar 25, 84, 89
Caesarea 23, 25, 61, 70, 72, 91
Cana of Galilee 86
Canonicity of Gospels 36–37
Carlson, Stephen C. 46
Carrington, P. 62–63
Chapman, J. H. 45
Chiliasts of Egypt 87
Christ. *See also* Jesus.
  Deity of 31, 32, 69, 87
  Prophecies concerning 66–67,
    68–69
Christians
  Gentile 32, 33, 61, 71, 83, 90,
    91
  Jewish 31, 33, 41, 54, 62–63,
    69–72
Church
  Community 8, 63, 69–70
  Early 35, 53, 90
  Expansion of 15–33
  Gentiles in 20–25, 60–62,
    65–68, 90
  Jerusalem 15–20, 60–61,
    66–67, 69–71, 84, 85, 89, 91
Cicero 84

Circumcision issue 20–21, 71
Clement of Alexandria 38, 40, 41, 42, 43, 45, 46, 48, 52, 60, 76–77, 84, 88
Cleopas 17
Codex Vaticanus 65
Codices 27
Colossians 25, 61
Commentaries, early 29, 87
Community discourse 20
Conflation of Matthew/Luke in Mark 56, 57
Coptic version 87
Cornelius 21
Council of Jerusalem. *See* Jerusalem.
Criticism, Bible 14, 18, 40, 44, 52–53, 57–59, 71. *See also* Historical-critical method.
Cyprus 25

Damascus 21, 54
Daniel 69
David 17, 19, 68
Death of Christ 13, 16, 30, 69, 72, 90, 91
Dependence issues 37
Dialogue with Trypho. See Justin Martyr.
Diaspora 16
Dionysius of Alexandria 87
Discourse Analysis 57
Domitian 89

Egypt 39, 40, 41, 42, 87
Ellis, E. Earle 55
Emmaus 17
Enlightenment 14, 35–36, 53
Ephesus 30, 38, 88, 89, 92
Epiphanius 87
Eschatological discourse 20

Europe 36, 42, 47
Eusebius 37, 40, 41, 89
Eyewitness accounts 16, 25, 27, 29, 35, 50, 53, 57, 76–77, 83–84

Faith in Christ 13
Farmer, William 8, 9, 58
Fellowship in church 17
Form criticism 48, 53
Formation of Gospels 13–33
Fourfold Gospel Hypothesis 9–10, 14–15, 35, 46, 47, 51–53, 57–58, 59–63, 70, 72, 94, 90, 94
France 36

Galatians 22, 69
Galilean ministry 19, 24, 28–29, 73, 74, 75, 80–82
Galilee 72, 86
Gaul 88
Genealogies 41, 46, 67, 68–69, 72, 77
Gentiles, mission to 15, 20–30, 69, 70–71, 83, 90, 91. *See also* Christians, Gentile.
Germany 36
Gnosticism 31–32
God-fearers 20
Good Samaritan 83
Gospels
   Form of 18–19, 22–33
   Historicity 48
   Meaning of 14, 15–17
   Order of 29, 33, 43, 46, 47–59, 63, 85, 91, 92, 93, 94
   Origins of 35–63, 65–91
   Studies 7–9
Greco-Roman culture 46, 48, 72–73

Greece. *See* Achaia; Greco-Roman
  culture.
Greek text 18–19, 21, 48, 54, 65,
  68
Griesbach Hypothesis 8, 51
Griesbach, J. J. 56–57, 62, 76, 77

Hebrew 50, 72
Hellenistic
Hengel, M. 28
Heresies 37, 89
Hierapolis 40, 45, 88
High Priest
  Jesus as 85
  Jewish 17, 31
Higher criticism. *See* Criticism,
  Bible; Historical-critical
  method.
Historical-critical method 7–9, 48
Historicity of Gospels 8–9, 93–94
Holy Spirit 68, 90
  Inspiration of 15–23, 31, 39,
    40, 41, 88, 90

Inscripturation 13–33
Interpreter, Mark as 44, 49
Irenaeus 9, 14–15, 38, 42, 46, 49,
  87, 88, 89
Italy 39

James, Apostle 22, 61
James of Jerusalem 72
Jericho 74
Jerome 42, 44, 46, 50
Jerusalem 21, 23, 31, 46, 73, 74,
  82
  Church of 15–20, 33, 60–61,
    67, 69–70, 75–76, 84, 85, 89,
    90, 91
  Council 22

Jesus
  Death/resurrection of 13, 16,
    30, 69, 90, 91
  Genealogy of 17, 19, 41, 46,
    66–67, 68–69, 72, 77
  Gospel of 14, 16–20, 66–92
  High priesthood of 85
  Historical 48
  Ministry of 13–20, 25–26, 28,
    29, 31, 33, 35, 55, 60–61, 62,
    67, 90, 91
  Sayings of 43, 51, 68, 74
John, Apostle 22, 61, 65, 72, 87,
  89
John, Gospel of 14, 30–33, 85–90
  Purpose of 31–32, 33
  Supplemental nature of 15, 92
  Testimony regarding 38, 39,
    42, 44–45, 65–66
  Vocabulary of 14
John Mark, 16, 25, 26, 38–59, 65–
  66, 77, 91. *See also* Mark,
  Gospel of.
John the Baptist 17, 29, 53, 73,
  68–69, 78
Jonah 69
Joseph 19, 68
Judaism, church and 16, 17, 22
Judea 72
Judeo-Christian community 54
Justin Martyr 37–38, 44, 65

Knights, Caesar's 38, 45, 59, 77
Koine. See Greek text.
Kümmel, Werner 43
Kürzinger, J. 45, 50

Latin translations 65
Law of Moses 22, 66, 67, 69, 71
Lessing, Gotthold 36
Levites 17

Literary criticism 18, 52
Lord's Prayer 51
Luke 8, 61, 65-66
　Gospel of 14, 23-24, 25, 27,
　　28-29, 30, 44, 60, 69-70,
　　78-84
　Investigation of 23, 26
　Marcionite version of 37
　Order of 43, 46, 50, 85, 91
　Purpose of 32, 33, 62, 90, 91
　Testimony regarding 38, 39,
　　41-42, 49, 65-66
　Use of Matthew in 69-76

Marcion 37, 38, 49
Mark, Gospel of 14, 41, 76-85.
　See also John Mark.
　Ending of 30
　Extra detail of 56
　First Commentary on 29
　Order of 29, 33, 46, 47-59, 63,
　　91, 92, 93, 94
　Purpose of 26-30, 32, 33,
　　60-62, 90
　Testimony regarding 37-42,
　　43-46, 65-66
　Use of Matthew, Luke in 60
Mary 19, 24, 68
Matthew, apostle 18, 19, 41, 53,
　65-66
Matthew, Gospel of 17-20, 31-33,
　49, 50, 51, 57, 66-85, 86
　Kingdom in 14
　Luke's use of 25-30, 69-76
　Priority of 22-24, 44, 46, 47,
　　54-56, 59-63, 90-91, 93-94
　Purpose of 33, 67-68
　Testimony regarding 38-39,
　　41, 42, 43, 65-66
Matthias, Gospel of 39
Mediterranean

Messiah, Jesus as 15, 19, 31, 72,
　85
Messianic prophecy 17, 67, 69
Missionary
　Discourse 20
　Journeys of Paul 21-26
Monarchian Prologue 89-90
Muratorian
　Canon 46
　Fragment 39, 88

Nazareth 80
New Testament Greek. See Greek.
North Africa 42

Old Latin
　Prologue 39
　Version 65, 87
Old Testament 15, 43, 67
Oral tradition 26, 35, 55, 57, 62,
　66-67
Orchard, Bernard 8-10
Origen 38, 41-42, 50, 87-88

Palestinian origin of Matthew 19
Papias of Hierapolis 18, 40, 41,
　43, 44, 45, 50, 72, 84, 88
Papyri 48
Parables 51
　Discourse 20
Patmos 89
Patristic Witnesses 37-49, 65
Paul 55, 66, 68, 69, 71, 94
　Church leadership of 15,
　　46-47, 59-62, 75-76
　Gentile evangelism of 15,
　　20-25, 84-85
　Luke's Gospel and 26, 29, 32,
　　33, 38, 43, 44, 49, 50,
　　69-72, 90, 91
　Writings of 35, 42

INDEX

Pax Romana 16
Pentecost 16, 90
Perga 25
Persecution 20, 21, 89, 91
Peter 55, 61, 62, 68, 70, 72, 78,
    83–84, 85, 89, 90, 91, 92
    As Markan lecturer 25–33, 41,
        42–44,46, 49–51, 59–63, 66,
        76–85, 91
    Church leadership of 15, 16,
        21–23, 46–47, 59, 67, 75–76
    Inspiration of 8
    Testimony regarding 38, 42–44
Pharisees 17, 22, 67–68, 75, 83
Philemon 25, 61
Phrygia 88
Polycarp 88
Praetorian Guard 26, 45, 59, 77,
    84
Presbyter 45
Proto-Matthew 43

Q 24–25, 43, 53–54
Qumran 55

Rabbinic interpretation 67
Rationalism 7–8
Reddish, M. G. 55
Reimarus, Hermann 36
Resurrection 13, 15, 16, 27, 29,
    53, 78, 79, 83–84, 89, 90, 91
Revelation 87, 89
Richards, E. R. 27
Riley, Harold 60
Robinson, J. A. T. 59
Roman. *See also* Greco-Roman
    culture; Praetorian Guard.
    Empire 16, 18, 21, 23, 25, 36,
        45, 48, 59, 76, 91
    Phase 15, 25–32
Romans, Epistle to 22

Rome 46
Rousseau, Jean-Jacques 36

Sadducees 17, 67
Savior, Jesus as 85
Sayings
    of Jesus 43, 51, 68, 74
    Source. *See* Q.
Scribes 67, 75, 83
Scrolls 18, 27, 78
Semitisms 19
Septuagint 15–16, 18–19
Sermon
    Of Matthew 19–20
    On the Mount 19–20, 51, 73,
        74
    On the Plain 73
Sherwin-White, A. N. 48
Simon the Sorcerer 40
Solomon 69
Source criticism 53, 54, 56–57,
    87, 94. *See also* Fourfold Gospel
    Hypothesis.
Stephen 21
Streeter, B. H. 51, 59
Suffering servant of Isaiah 17
Supplement, Johannine 15,
    30–32
Synoptic
    Gospels 30–31, 46–47, 63
    Problem 14, 51–58, 77, 93–94
Syrian version 87

Taylor, R. O. P. 45
Tertullian 38
Tetramorphon Gospel 14–15
Theophilus of Antioch 88
Thessalonians 20, 69
Thomas, Gospel of 39
Titus 42
Torah. *See* Law of Moses.

Tradition
    From early church 18, 29, 30,
        58–59, 85, 87–88, 93
    Of Gospels 32, 35, 37–47, 49,
        59, 65–68
    Oral 26, 70
Transmission, oral 55
Tuckett, C. M. 59
Turner, E. G. 48
Two-Gospel Hypothesis 8–9, 47

Vatican II 9
Virgin birth. *See* Birth of Christ.
Voltaire, François Marie 36

Watson, F. 14
Widow's mite 83

Zachaeus 82